CRUCIFIED PEOPLE

CRUCIFIED PEOPLE

The Suffering of the Tortured in Today's World

John Neafsey

ORBIS BOOKS

Maryknoll, New York 10545

Founded in 1970, Orbis Books endeavors to publish works that enlighten the mind, nourish the spirit, and challenge the conscience. The publishing arm of the Maryknoll Fathers and Brothers, Orbis seeks to explore the global dimensions of the Christian faith and mission, to invite dialogue with diverse cultures and religious traditions, and to serve the cause of reconciliation and peace. The books published reflect the views of their authors and do not represent the official position of the Maryknoll Society. To learn more about Maryknoll and Orbis Books, please visit our website at www.maryknollsociety.org.

Manuscript editing and typesetting by Joan Weber Laflamme.

ISBN 978-1-62698-068-6

Library of Congress Cataloging-in-Publication Data

Neafsey, John.
Crucified people : the suffering of the tortured in today's world / John Neafsey.
    pages cm
    ISBN 978-1-62698-068-6 (pbk.)
    1. Suffering—Religious aspects—Christianity. 2. Torture—Religious aspects—Christianity. I. Title.
BV4909.N38 2014
261.8'3315—dc23

                                                                    2013037405

We are disciples of one who was tortured.
—Paolo Ricca

Human beings suffer,
they torture one another,
they get hurt and get hard.
No poem or play or song
can fully right a wrong
inflicted or endured.

The innocent in gaols
beat on their bars together.
A hunger-striker's father
stands in the graveyard dumb.
The police widow in veils
faints at the funeral home.

History says, Don't hope
on this side of the grave.
But then, once in a lifetime
the longed for tidal wave
of justice can rise up,
and hope and history rhyme.

So hope for a great sea-change
on the far side of revenge.
Believe that a further shore
is reachable from here.
Believe in miracles
and cures and healing wells.
—Seamus Heaney, *The Cure at Troy*

CONTENTS

PREFACE

The center of the world—so called because the crucified Jesus dwells there, and with him all who suffer unjustly, all the poor and despised of the earth—is the place from which we must proclaim the risen Lord.

—Gustavo Gutiérrez[1]

FOR MANY YEARS, the Church of the Holy Sepulchre has been a recurring image in my dreams. This place of pilgrimage in the Old City of Jerusalem houses both the place of crucifixion and the place of resurrection. Here is found the tragic end of the Via Dolorosa: Golgotha, the Place of the Skull, where Jesus and countless others who got into trouble with the imperial authorities were taken to be publicly tortured to death. Here also is the empty tomb of Jesus, the actual Holy Sepulchre. Early on, this place of trauma and sorrow became a holy place, a sacred destination to which pilgrims would come from all over the world to draw inspiration and strength for living.[2]

Over thirty years ago I made my own pilgrimage to Jerusalem. The day after my arrival I wandered the narrow streets of the Old City, beginning in the Muslim Quarter and following the traditional path of the stations of the cross all the way to the ancient courtyard of the Church of the Holy Sepulchre. But instead of the wide-eyed awe and reverence befitting a pilgrim, my nose was in a tourist guidebook, wanting to be sure I didn't miss any of the big sights.

Suddenly, a voice caught my attention: "Can I help you, man?" Curiously, the accent was more reminiscent of the South Side of my hometown of Chicago than the Middle East. When I looked up, I met the haunting eyes of an unforgettable character: a slight, emaciated, unkempt man whose energy and spirit, nonetheless, were of biblical proportions. His name was Samuel. He was African American, a Vietnam veteran, a US Marine who had been severely wounded in a fire fight with the Viet Cong about ten years prior. During a long period of painful convalescence in stateside VA hospitals, he had resolved to use his veteran's disability benefits to subsidize the remainder of his life on earth as a perpetual spiritual pilgrim—fasting, praying, wandering among the holy places, performing works of mercy. He picked up his monthly disability check at the Jerusalem post office.

It turned out that I was to be Samuel's work of mercy that afternoon. "What are you looking for?" he asked. "I'd like to see the Hill of Calvary," I answered. The ascetic fellow admonished me: "Man, don't look at that book! Let your *heart* guide you!" He beckoned me to follow, and I sheepishly did so, as he set off up an ancient stairway inside the church. When we reached the summit, he led me to a mandala inlaid into the marble floor of a chapel richly adorned with Greek Orthodox iconography, incense burners, and religious paraphernalia. "You see this?" he said, pointing to the mandala. "This is the *center of the world!*" Then he led me to a gold-plated hole underneath an altar just a few steps away, beside which it was possible to see the actual rock of Golgotha under glass. Then, in a hushed, reverent tone: "And you see *this*? This is the place where the cross went down." Samuel then dropped to his knees on the floor. My knees seemed to buckle reflexively and, in a moment, I found myself kneeling alongside this eccentric holy man at the place of the crucifixion, my eyes and heart now wide open, awed by the terrible, redemptive beauty at the center of the world.

The center of the world, sometimes referred to as the *axis mundi*, is a universal mythic image encountered across many religious and spiritual traditions through the ages.[3] Black Elk, an Oglala Lakota Sioux holy man and healer from the western plains of the United

States—who himself lived through a kind of crucifixion of his own people in the latter part of the nineteenth century—described a remarkable vision he had as a young boy. In the vision he was taken to a high mountain that was similarly revealed to him as the center of the world. He later came to believe that the actual mountain in his vision was Harney Peak, the highest point in the Black Hills of South Dakota, a place of great sacredness for his people. He stated, significantly, "But *anywhere* is the center of the world."[4]

From a Christian perspective the actual place where the cross went down was certainly hallowed for all time by the redemptive suffering of Jesus on that sad Friday in first-century Jerusalem, causing it to become, for Christians, the center of the world. Perhaps the deeper spiritual lesson, though, is to recognize that the center of the world is *anywhere* a cross goes down, that Christ suffers *wherever* human beings are tortured and disrespected, and *whenever* they are treated as less than sacred. The historical Jesus was certainly tortured there and then, two thousand years ago at the Place of the Skull, but Christ *continues* to suffer, here and now, in the unjust suffering of the innocent. New crosses are raised all the time all over our twenty-first century world. We seem to be caught in the unholy grip of what Freud would call a *repetition compulsion*—in our case, to reenact the barbaric cruelty of the crucifixion with new victims every day.

I am grateful to Gwyneth Leech for permission to use her haunting painting of the tenth station of the cross, "Jesus Is Stripped of His Garments," on the cover of this book. It is one of a series of fourteen stations of the cross she was commissioned to paint for St. Paul's on the Green, an Episcopal church in Norwalk, Connecticut, where they were permanently installed in March 2005. "My brief," she writes, "was to reimagine the traditional iconography in contemporary terms."[5] The question that guided her work: "How could I make the Passion narrative real to a present-day congregation, how could I make it a story for our time, our generation?"[6]

Although she was unsure what particular modern form the paintings would take when she took on the project, it turned out that tragic photographs from the Iraq War became her inspiration; a newspaper photo of Iraqi women grieving for a car-bomb victim set in motion a flow of connections that helped her to reimagine the grieving women along the Via Dolorosa. But it was the collection of horrible photos of tortured Iraqi prisoners from Abu Ghraib prison, first made public in May 2004, that triggered the most striking and controversial connections between the crucifixion of Jesus and victims of torture in the contemporary world. Leech acknowledges that the source image for "Jesus Is Stripped of His Garments" was the photo of the naked, terrified Iraqi prisoner being menaced by ferocious US military dogs at Abu Ghraib.

Leech writes:

> When the photos from Abu Ghraib prison appeared, other parts of the Passion story had a new resonance for me. The Romans stripped the condemned and crucified them naked as a way of utterly humiliating them and breaking their spirits. Here were dozens of images of modern prisoners stripped naked for the same reasons. I decided to compose the tenth station with the man threatened by dogs, echoing Psalm 22, sung each Good Friday: "Deliver me, Lord, from the mouth of the dog."[7]

My hope is that this book will make "cross connections" with words just as Gwyneth Leech makes them with her paintings, and that they will evoke similar associations to the meaning of the cross in the context of the contemporary world. I want to do this not only by linking the pain of torture here and now with the pain of crucifixion there and then, but by searching for redemptive potential anywhere that crosses go down, anywhere that crosses are raised, anywhere that crucified people are trying to survive, heal, and rise again.

I'm sending out thanks in all directions. Robert Ellsberg at Orbis Books is a gem. His patience, encouragement, and consistently gracious attitude through all the ups and downs of writing this book have been a gift. I am honored and humbled that this book will be included in the Orbis canon.

I'm ever grateful to my wife, Maura, for her loving support, day in and day out, all through the long gestation of this book. Thanks also to my son, Bryan, and my daughter, Rosie, for their patience with me as I pecked away on my laptop. I know they are looking forward to Dad being a little more fun now that the book is done!

Thanks also to the staff members at the Heartland Alliance Marjorie Kovler Center for allowing me the opportunity to work with them at the old convent they have turned into a sanctuary for the tortured in Chicago. Finally, gratitude and blessings to the survivors we serve at Kovler Center. It is a privilege to be in the presence of such brave and resilient people. This book is for them.

INTRODUCTION

In prison cell and dungeon vile,
our thoughts to them go winging,
When friends by shame are undefiled,
how can I keep from singing?
—Doris Plenn[1]

BEFORE TELLING THEIR sad stories at public events on the issue of torture, some survivors of torture begin by lighting a candle
in remembrance of people who have been tortured, especially for
those who are being tortured right now. This ritual is a way of
bringing light to dark places we would rather forget, a practice of
"dangerous memory," of sending solidarity on the wings of prayer
to people under torment by other human beings. It is a way of af-
firming that human beings are sacred and of reminding ourselves
that they should be treated as such. My hope is that this book will
be like such a candle of mourning and remembrance.

A number of formative experiences and influences have inspired
and shaped this book. First, and most compelling, has been my
privilege to work as a psychologist with men and women who are
survivors of torture. About twelve years ago I decided to volunteer
my services as a therapist at the Heartland Alliance Marjorie Kovler
Center, a program that serves immigrant survivors of torture in the
Chicago area. For several years this involved providing pro bono
psychotherapy for torture survivors for an hour or two each week,
along with facilitating a group for graduate psychology and social
work student trainees who were learning to work with survivors—

which necessarily includes learning to understand and work with the challenging feelings that traumatized people evoke in their helpers. Three years ago I was offered a position as a staff psychologist at the Kovler Center, and with some trepidation, I decided to join its team at the old convent it has turned into a sanctuary for the tortured in the Rogers Park neighborhood of Chicago.[2]

One of my job responsibilities is to conduct intake evaluations of torture survivors who are seeking help for the first time. This intensive process usually involves at least three or four in-depth interviews, which include exploring the experiences of torture and persecution that led them to flee their country. In order to know their present needs, we must also learn about their current circumstances, which are often precarious and sometimes desperate.

Survivors inevitably pour out their stories in heartbreaking, excruciating detail. All are suffering from some painful combination of depression and post-traumatic stress. Some have lasting physical injuries or medical conditions caused by their torture. Most sleep poorly, their nights disturbed by anxiety and nightmares, their waking hours often plagued by haunting memories and traumatic imagery of things they wish they could forget. Most have no money, no job, no health insurance. Many have little or no social support. The lucky have secure places to live with family members or kind people from their country of origin who provide hospitality and sanctuary, but many do the best they can in less-than-ideal situations, sleeping on floors or couches in homes of people who are willing to let them stay for a while. Some end up in homeless shelters. Many have multiple pressing needs for medical and psychiatric care, food, housing, case management, psychotherapy, and legal services. In spite of all of the above, the Kovler staff members are often awed by the remarkable resilience and courage of the people we serve. We are humbled too by their kindness and courtesy and patience with us.

The demographics of the people who come to Kovler Center are quite diverse and vary according to trouble spots in the world and immigration patterns in Chicago at any given time. When the center was founded in the late 1980s, most came from Latin America—in especially large numbers from El Salvador and Guatemala with their brutal, repressive governments and violent civil wars. These days the largest percentage of people we serve come from East, Central, and West Africa, along with significant numbers from various countries in the Middle East, Asia, Eastern Europe, and Latin America. Some speak English, but many don't, and so we often work with language interpreters (French, Arabic, Amharic, and Tigrinya are in greatest demand at the present time). Most are in the process of applying for political asylum in the United States—a complex, emotionally demanding, uncertain legal process that can sometimes take years. Survivors must present testimony and evidence to convince skeptical immigration judges and asylum officers that they have a "well-founded fear" of further persecution and harm if they should return to their country.

I want to ground this book, as much as possible, in the life stories and personal experiences of real people who have suffered torture. To protect the confidentiality and privacy of any survivors I have known personally, I take pains to disguise carefully any identifying information from their personal histories or countries of origin, sometimes creating composite profiles to ensure anonymity. I also draw widely from a diverse sampling of the personal testimonies of survivors who have written or spoken publicly about their experiences in autobiographies, memoirs, films, interviews, and human rights reports. For some survivors, the act of telling their story— often in the context of speaking out against torture—has become an important part of their ongoing journey of healing and recovery.

Some of these accounts of torture are shocking and painful to read, with the result that some readers will run the risk of "vicarious traumatization" even by learning about such experiences second-hand. My advice to those who find themselves feeling overwhelmed or depressed is to put the book down and take a break for as long as is needed. But do try to come back when you are able. The pain and anguish of torture are real, and so, for the sake of the tortured, we must allow ourselves to take this painful reality into our consciousness as best we can. This includes learning to tolerate the uncomfortable feelings that torture evokes in us. The tortured—and all those at risk of torture now and in times to come—need us to hear their pain, their need, their cries for help. They also need us to act on their behalf, but first we need to *listen*.

In the words of Jon Sobrino, we must learn to "hear the word of reality."[3] By this he means particularly the reality of needless, unjust suffering. Sobrino says the natural response of the human heart to injustice and inhumanity always consists of some combination of *compassion* and *indignation*. Compassion is the feeling that stirs within us when we are touched or moved by the need or suffering of others. Indignation, on the other hand, is a kind of holy anger or outrage we feel for people who suffer needlessly and unjustly. These feelings are always accompanied by inclinations toward action—compassion by the wish to *do* something to relieve the pain, and indignation by the wish to *change* or *remove* the unjust conditions that are causing the hurt in the first place. Callings to service and justice originate in these stirrings of compassion and indignation in our heart, and so our heart's response to the reality of torture can give us clues to what we are called to do about it.

On a deeper level there is a way that the response of our own hearts can put us in touch with the heart of God. The feelings that torture evokes in us can help us to know something of God's grief and heartache and heartbreak over how badly so many of his children are being treated in this world. Listening to the reality of the tortured can also help us to hear what God is trying to tell us through their pain and need. "If reality speaks and God can speak in it," says Sobrino, "especially when it cries out, then listening to it is a necessary way of realizing our humanity."[4]

Other important formative influences are Ignatian spirituality and liberation theology, with a special interest in the practical implications of these for vocational discernment and self-discovery. My first book, *A Sacred Voice Is Calling*, was an interdisciplinary exploration of vocation and social responsibility informed by modern psychology, Ignatian spirituality, and liberation theology. This book draws from similar wells of wisdom and inspiration.[5] Although vocational discernment is often seen as applying rather narrowly to our choice of work or career, it can also be understood more broadly to include discernment of what we are called to do in response to particular social issues or circumstances that arise in the life of our local or national or global communities. These might include the reckless wars our country starts in places like Iraq and Afghanistan, torture, poverty, racism, expanding global inequity and injustice, immigration, waste and overconsumption of resources, destruction of the environment, or any other issue that calls upon us to rise to the occasion, to take a stand, to take a risk, to do the right thing.

On a personal level, the issue of torture has exerted a strong "moral tug" upon my heart.[6] This was especially heightened by my travels to Central America, the heartbreak and desperation and traumatic history of that area of the world, and the haunting awareness of my own country's dark role in promoting and facilitating injustice and violent repression in places like El Salvador, Guatemala, Nicaragua, and Honduras. Jennifer Harbury's powerful book, *Truth, Torture, and the American Way,* offers a harrowing historical documentation of clandestine US involvement in torture in Latin America and elsewhere for decades prior to the shameless, unapologetic, public promotion of torture by the Bush administration in the years following the 9/11 attacks.[7]

My work with survivors of torture has also heightened my personal sense of grief and shame and anger in response to the scandals over maltreatment of prisoners in the custody of US military and intelligence services at places like Abu Ghraib in Iraq, Bagram Air Force Base in Afghanistan, and Guantanamo Bay, Cuba. As a psychologist, I was particularly embarrassed by numerous reports of fellow psychologists "consulting" with interrogators in such places, including some evidence of direct involvement in guiding or monitoring torture sessions. Incredibly, even after these disclosures, the leadership of the American Psychological Association (APA) gave its official blessing to the continued involvement of psychologists in coercive interrogations of "unlawful enemy combatants" at illegal detention centers in places like Guantanamo Bay, which has become a global symbol of injustice and cruelty. This led to widespread dissent among the APA membership, including a group of several hundred psychologists who withheld professional dues in protest; some of us eventually resigned when it became clear that the leadership was largely unresponsive to our concerns.[8]

In these dark post-9/11 times of pre-emptive war, "enhanced interrogation," "extraordinary rendition," and extrajudicial execution by unmanned drones, I have found that returning to my Christian roots—and especially to the cross—has been a source of consolation and reorientation again and again. Remembering the cross has helped me to meditate more concretely on the life of Jesus, who, after all, was himself a Middle Eastern man who was tortured to death by the forces of an occupying army in his own country.

An imaginative prayer exercise suggested by Saint Ignatius Loyola is quite powerful; he suggests that we place ourselves in our mind's eye before the crucified Jesus and then "ponder upon what presents itself to our mind" as we consider a number of questions:

What have I done for Christ? What am I doing for Christ? What ought I to do for Christ? As I behold Christ in this plight, nailed to the cross, I shall ponder upon what presents itself to my mind.[9]

But the exercise can also be turned around, beginning not with the crucified Jesus of the past, but rather with suffering people in the contemporary world. In the spirit of the saint who was his namesake, Ignacio Ellacuría suggested an alternative imaginative exercise. He advised that we begin our contemplation with the grim present-day realities faced by the multitudes he referred to as the "crucified people" of the world:

I want you to set your eyes and your hearts on these peoples who are suffering so much—some from poverty and hunger, others from oppression and repression. Then . . . standing before this people thus crucified you must repeat St. Ignatius' examination from the first week of the *Exercises*. Ask yourselves: What have I done to crucify them? What do I do to uncrucify them? What must I do for this people to rise again?[10] The challenge is to see where this kind of "Christic imagination" takes us as we consider the cross in our twenty-first-century context.[11]

This book is the fruit of my own efforts to ponder these things, including the promptings of conscience that seem to inevitably arise in the course of such contemplation. Before the realities of torture and the cross, an uneasy conscience is perhaps the best place to begin.

1

TORTURE AND THE CROSS

Christ Suffers in Ten Thousand Places

Crosses keep on being set up in the world; the cry of abandonment echoes down through the centuries.
— Elizabeth Johnson[1]

How Calvary in Palestine,
Extending down to me and mine,
Was but the first leaf in a line
Of trees on which a Man could swing
World without end, in suffering
For all men's healing, let me sing.
— Countee Cullen[2]

"CHRIST PLAYS IN ten thousand places," wrote Gerard Manley Hopkins, "Lovely in limbs, and lovely in eyes not his."[3] Sadly, we can also say that Christ suffers in ten thousand places, is crucified in ten thousand places; lovely limbs contorted in pain, fear and anguish in lovely eyes—not his—down through the centuries, even at this very moment, in dark, lonely, scary places all around the world.

In this chapter I explore the relationship of the cross and torture, the suffering of Christ and the suffering of people. I'll begin with the historical Jesus, with what Johann Baptist Metz has called the "dangerous memory" of the crucified Jesus. But the tortured Jesus cannot be remembered without his many companions—the community of the tortured. Past and present, living and dead, they know, like him, what it is like to suffer unjustly. In the face of such suffering and evil it becomes necessary to wrestle with the humbling, faith-challenging question: Where is God?

THE TORTURE OF JESUS

The Gospels were not written as historical documents, but we can be fairly certain that a man named Jesus of Nazareth was crucified in Jerusalem on a Friday afternoon in the spring of a year sometime between AD 26 and 36, the period when Pontius Pilate was the procurator of Roman-occupied Judea, during the reign of Tiberius Caesar.[4] "He was crucified under Pontius Pilate" became the grim historical "factoid" in the Nicene Creed to help Christians remember that Jesus was tortured to death in a particular way in a particular time and place.

It is highly unlikely that Jesus' followers would invent the tragic, off-putting story of his public torture and execution. One way New Testament scholars assess the historical probability of certain stories or sayings in the Gospels is the *criterion of embarrassment,* which involves consideration of whether including them (versus softening or suppressing them) could potentially have embarrassed or created difficulties for the early church.[5] The crucifixion of Jesus by the Romans certainly meets this criterion, because crucifixion was widely regarded in the ancient world as a shameful death, a punishment for slaves or revolutionaries. This is why the inclusion of this dark story is suggestive of greater authenticity and historical probability.

There are also two early and independent non-Christian accounts of the crucifixion of Jesus, one Roman and one Jewish. Early in the second century a Roman historian, Publius Cornelius Tacitus, wrote these disdainful lines about Jesus and his followers:

Christus, from whom the name had its origin, suffered the extreme penalty during the reign of Tiberias at the hands of one of our procurators, Pontius Pilatus, and a most mischievous superstition, thus checked for the moment, again broke out, not only in Judea, the first source of the evil, but even in Rome, where all things hideous and shameful from every part of the world find their centre and become popular.[6]

And Flavius Josephus, a Jewish historian writing even earlier, around AD 90, wrote this:

At this time appeared Jesus, a wise man. For he was one who wrought surprising feats and was a teacher of such people as accept the truth gladly. He won over many Jews and many of the Greeks. When Pilate, upon hearing him accused by men of the highest standing among us, had condemned him to be crucified, those who had in the first place come to love him did not give up their affection for him. . . . And the tribe of Christians, so called after him, has still to this day not disappeared.[7]

The Gospels suggest that Pontius Pilate suffered from a guilty conscience about executing Jesus, and that he did so only reluctantly to placate Jewish authorities and the bloodthirsty Jerusalem mob. Tragically, these passages became the foundation and justification for later Christian anti-Judaism and racist anti-Semitism.[8] Other ancient accounts, however, give a very different picture of Pilate, suggesting that he had few qualms about violent repression of dissent and resistance to Roman occupation, and that he had a reputation for excessive cruelty and brutality (even by Roman imperial standards).[9] Philo of Alexandria, another Jewish writer who lived at the time of Jesus, described Pilate as "inflexible, merciless, and obstinate."[10] He offered this list of Pilate's crimes: "bribery, tyranny, pillage, violence, calumny, constant execution without passing a verdict, and endless,

insufferable cruelty."[11] Paula Fredriksen concludes that "Pilate's reported conduct as reluctant judge is scarcely credible as history."[12]

Crucifixion was an unusually cruel method of torture and execution used by the Romans and other ancient peoples. "To force
a condemned prisoner to drag through a jeering crowd the instrument that will shortly be used to torture him to death," writes Susan
Nieman, "is a refinement of cruelty that ought to take your breath
away."[13] I will not dwell on the gruesome details and variations of
this practice, which Martin Hengel describes as "an utterly offensive
affair, 'obscene' in the original sense of the word," in his scholarly
historical review, *Crucifixion in the Ancient World and the Folly of the
Message of the Cross.*[14]

The mechanics of crucifixion are less important than the func-
tions it served. First, it was the ultimate form of capital punishment
for individual offenders, being reserved especially for lower-class
people who were thought to be a threat to imperial law and order.
Second, and perhaps most important for our purposes, crucifixion
was a method of social deterrence used to "keep the peace" by terrifying unhappy colonized peoples into submission. Here is Hengel's
summary:

> Crucifixion was and remained a political and military punish-
> ment. . . . Among the Romans it was inflicted above all on
> the lower classes, i.e., slaves, violent criminals, and the unruly
> elements in rebellious provinces, not least in Judea.
>
> The chief reason for its use was its allegedly supreme ef-
> ficacy as a deterrent; it was, of course, carried out publicly.
> . . . At the same time, crucifixion satisfied the primitive lust
> for revenge and sadistic cruelty of individual rulers and of the
> masses. It was usually associated with other forms of torture,
> including at least flogging. At relatively small expense and to
> great public effect the criminal could be tortured to death
> for days in an unspeakable way. . . . By the public display of
> the naked victim at a prominent place—at a crossroads, in the

theatre, on high ground, at the place of his crime—crucifixion
also represented his uttermost humiliation. . . . Crucifixion
was aggravated further by the fact that quite often its victims
were never buried. It was a stereotyped picture that the crucified victim served as food for wild beasts and birds of prey. In
this way his humiliation was made complete.[15]

There are a number of historical accounts of mass crucifixion by
Roman imperial forces, including the crucifixion of thousands of
rebels along the Appian Way outside Rome during the slave rebel-
lion led by Spartacus between 73 and 71 BC, and the crucifixion
of as many as two thousand Jewish rebels outside Jerusalem by
Publius Quintilius Varus, the Roman governor of Syria, in 4 BC.
Just a few decades after Jesus' death, during the siege of Jerusalem by
Roman forces in AD 70, Josephus himself was an eyewitness to the
crucifixion of hundreds of starving Jews who desperately ventured
outside the walls in search of food:

The majority were citizens of the poorer class. . . . When
caught, they were . . . scourged and subjected to torture of
every description . . . and then crucified opposite the walls . . .
five hundred or more being captured daily. . . . The soldiers
out of rage and hatred amused themselves by nailing their
prisoners in different postures; and so great was their number,
that space could not be found for the crosses nor crosses for
the bodies.[16]

For the purposes of this book it is less important to reiterate the
poignant stories and memorable dialogues contained in the passion
narratives, and more crucial to establish the historical fact and context of Jesus' crucifixion—Jesus being one among many victims of
a kind of state terrorism inflicted on nations and peoples subjugated
by imperial Rome. "It was not theologians, who invented the cross,"
writes Dorothee Soelle, "rather, the Roman Empire thought up

this method of deterring people who heard the cry for liberation by slowly and publicly torturing to death those who cried out."[17]

The *historical reality* of Jesus' crucifixion is important to liberation theologians not only to verify whether it really happened, but also because it helps us appreciate the oppressive, death-dealing reality of the social and political and religious forces with which Jesus had to contend—and which ultimately led to his torture and execution. In his influential essay "The Crucified People," Ignacio Ellacuría explains:

> The historic character of the death of Jesus entails, to begin with, that his death took place for historic reasons. . . . Jesus dies—is killed . . . because of the historic life he led, a life of deeds and words that those who represented and held the reins of the religious, socioeconomic, and political situation could not tolerate. That he was regarded as a blasphemer, one who was destroying the traditional religious order, one who upset the social structure, a political agitator, and so forth, is simply to recognize from quite distinct angles that the activity, word, and the very person of Jesus . . . were so assertive and so against the established order and basic institutions that they had to be punished by death.[18]

Ellacuría wants us to be *real* and *true* in our remembering and thinking of Jesus, the dangerous time and place in which he lived, the violent manner by which he died, and the reasons for which he was put to death. Such recollection and reflection is done not only for purposes of personal piety or spiritual edification, but also to consider its social relevance and application to our own times, our realities. Ellacuría himself is a model both inspiring and intimidating. Like Jesus, he too lived and worked in an extremely dangerous time and place: El Salvador in the 1970s and 1980s. He too took assertive public risks; in his case, on behalf of the traumatized poor of the troubled country that had become his home. And because of his option for the poor, he too was violently executed by the forces of an army that served the interests of the powerful ruling class.[19]

Ellacuría is just one example of the way serious reflection on how Jesus lived and died can be potentially quite risky and even dangerous, especially for those who take it to heart in how they choose to live their life. In some times and places, opting for the poor is a life-and-death matter. Archbishop Oscar Romero, a friend and mentor to Ellacuría, also paid the ultimate price of martyrdom for taking sides with the abused poor of El Salvador. Romero spoke these sobering words just a month before his assassination in March 1980: "Believe me, brothers and sisters, anyone committed to the poor must suffer the same fate as the poor. And in El Salvador we know the fate of the poor: to be taken away, to be tortured, to be jailed, to be found dead."[20] In a nutshell: Jesus lived with such integrity and love and courage in the face of danger that it got him tortured and killed—and some of his followers may be called to do the same.

Jesus had an edge. "This child is destined for the falling and the rising of many in Israel," were the words of the old man Simeon to Jesus' mother, "and to be a sign that will be opposed" (Lk 2:34). From the very beginning the Gospels portray Jesus as often in tension or conflict with those who were threatened by his prophetic criticism of them. "To some he preaches good news," says Sobrino, "but to others bad news; to some he shows compassion, and to still others he shows anger."[21] Every blessing ("Blessed are you who are poor") is accompanied by a complementary denunciation ("But *woe* to you who are rich") (Lk 6:20, 24). The assertiveness of Jesus is often absent or played down in one-sided portrayals of him that highlight his meekness, gentleness, and pacifism. We end up with a safe, conflict-avoiding, bourgeois Jesus with no "edges." The unfortunate consequence, says Sobrino, is that it "consciously or unconsciously influences us to avoid conflicts with those who continue oppressing the poor today, the successors to those who killed Jesus."[22]

In a similar vein Johann Baptist Metz writes of our stubborn, defensive, self-protective tendency to suppress or forget the memory of what he calls "the dangerous Christ": "The whole of history *anno Domino*, after Christ, may be interpreted as a maneuver to evade the dangerous Christ."[23] This Christ—the one with edges—can be evaded or forgotten for all kinds of reasons. His unsettling prophetic voice is easily shouted down or drowned out by the "great, boring, banal voice of mass culture."[24] In times when a majority of American Christians believe that torture is sometimes justified to protect national security, it is especially convenient for us to forget that "we are disciples of one who was tortured."[25]

It is also tempting for us to keep the ugly reality of torture and its victims—who are the present-day equivalents of the tortured Christ—out of sight and out of mind. It is to them that we turn next.

ONLY THE SUFFERING GOD CAN HELP

Jesus is one of uncounted millions of men and women who have suffered torture throughout history. They are linked to him and to each other by this God-forsaken experience. It makes for a kind of tragic solidarity of the tortured, a fragile but real communal lifeline between those who have been victimized—past and present, living and dead, those who survived and those who did not. "Jesus never comes alone," writes Paolo Ricca. "One cannot have him without having, along with him, his company, his community."[26] Eduardo Galeano says it this way: "Yes, indeed: however hurt and shattered one might be, one can always find contemporaries anywhere in time, and compatriots anywhere in space."[27]

Certain contemporary images and stories of torture have a kind of sad symmetry with the passion of Jesus. The photo of the hooded man at Abu Ghraib prison, perched on a box in his ragged cloak, wired up for electrical torture, arms outstretched in the posture of the crucified, has become the iconic image of torture in the twenty-first century.[28] It is hard not to think of the scourged, humiliated Jesus in his purple cloak as he was presented by Pilate to the jeering crowd: "Ecce Homo! Behold the Man!" (Jn 19:5). At Abu Ghraib, though, "the man" was an Iraqi, an "unlawful enemy combatant" to whom the Geneva Conventions did not apply.

Also eerily reminiscent of crucifixion is the 1998 image of the battered body of Matthew Shepard, a young gay man who suffered severe head injuries from beatings by homophobic thugs and who was then tied to a Wyoming fence and left to hang there to die. It was eighteen hours before his body was discovered.[29] Earlier the same year another gruesome passion play was enacted in Jasper, Texas, when an African American man named James Byrd Jr. was set upon by white men who beat him and urinated on him, chained him by his ankles to the back of a pickup truck, and then dragged him for three miles along an asphalt road until his head came off.[30] Christ as hate-crime victim.[31]

The horrifying photos of lynched African Americans, sometimes including their perpetrators and leering spectators, also evoke the grim spectacle of Golgotha.[32] But this time the cross was a lynching tree on which men and women were hung or burned alive, over and over, in Alabama, Georgia, Mississippi, Texas, and on across the nineteenth- and twentieth-century South. James Cone, the founding father of black liberation theology, has explored the disturbing parallels between lynching and crucifixion in his powerful book *The Cross and the Lynching Tree*.[33] In the same spirit Countee Cullen, a young poet of the Harlem Renaissance, wrote "Christ Recrucified" in 1922 at the height of the lynching era:

> The South is crucifying Christ again
> By all the laws of ancient rote and rule:
> The ribald cries of "Save Yourself" and "Fool"
> Din in his ears, the thorns grope for his brain
> And where they bite, swift springing rivers stain
> His gaudy, purple robe of ridicule

With sullen red; and acid wine to cool
His thirst is thrust at him with lurking pain.
Christ's awful wrong is that he's of darker hue,
The sin for which no blamelessness atones;
But lest the sameness of the cross should tire
They kill him now with famished tongues of fire,
And while he burns, good men, and women, too,
Shout, battling for his black and brittle bones.[34]

Paradoxically, the fact that Jesus was tortured can be a source of consolation to some torture survivors, who are able to experience, through him, something of what it feels like to be empathically understood or *known*: "Nobody knows the trouble I've seen, nobody knows but Jesus." This emotional connection with the tortured Christ can offer at least some relief—if not from suffering itself, at least from the crushing experience of bearing it alone.

Not all torture survivors, to be sure, are able to relate to Jesus. And yet, for some, the experience of torture has the potential to become a connecting lifeline of solidarity and compassion, however tenuous, with the crucified Christ. This can even apply to non-Christians. I am thinking of a Muslim woman from a Middle Eastern country who was kidnapped, raped, and tortured by extremist militants, and who thereafter suffered from such chronic emotional anguish that she rarely got a decent night of sleep. She once had a dream in which she had encountered *Isa* (Arabic for *Jesus*). In the dream Isa tenderly spoke the following message to her: "Don't worry, daughter, everything is going to be all right." She awakened feeling a profound sense of consolation and peace. The dream was not an occasion for miraculous healing or for conversion to Christianity; neither did it change her Muslim view of Jesus as one in a long line of great but nonetheless human prophets. But she did experience her dream visitor as someone who could reassure her, with great personal authority, that it is possible to recover a sense of personal dignity and peace after torture.

Jesus' unjust suffering makes it possible for people under similar circumstances to feel a connection with him. The crucified Jesus is someone with whom they can relate: a *human* God, a God who suffers, a compassionate God who is able to appreciate what it is like to be a suffering human being. The crucified Jesus also evokes compassion in *us* for the God who suffers, giving us a feeling for the radical vulnerability and helplessness of God. We are touched and moved by the pain of God; God feels for *us* and we feel for *God*.[35]

This also enables people to be *helped* by Jesus. Reinhold Schneider, an Austrian Catholic writer who was accused of treason by the Nazis, but who was spared because the war ended before he could be tried, had a mystical appreciation for this: "The one who suffers with us on earth . . . is more helpful than the risen one."[36] Dietrich Bonhoeffer shared a similar sentiment in one of is letters from prison prior to his execution by the Nazis:

> God lets himself be pushed out of the world on to the cross. He is weak and powerless in the world, and that is precisely the way, the only way, in which he is with us and helps us. . . . Only the suffering God can help.[37]

WHERE IS GOD?

The question of whether and where God can be found in the God-forsaken experience of torture must be approached with great care and humility. Cheap, easy answers to the problem of evil are of no help to anyone—especially to people who have been tortured.

In her reflections on the widespread problem of rape and physical abuse of women, Elizabeth Johnson seems to have found the proper tone. She uses the imagery of crucifixion to convey "the pain and violence experienced by women on the cross, of whatever sort." She is profoundly skeptical and cautious: "There is no solution here, no attempt at a theoretical reconciliation of atrocity with divine will. Only a terrible sense of the mystery of evil and the absence of God, which nevertheless may betray divine presence, desecrated."[38]

God *absent*. Or, if present at all, *desecrated*. This kind of theology seems more promising in approaching the evil of torture. It also feels more congruent with the gospel accounts of Jesus' anguished cry from the cross: "My God, my God, why have you forsaken me?" (Mk 15:34; Mt 27:46). Here we have the impossible mystery of the crucified God, utterly helpless, abandoned to suffer torture and a miserable death alone.

Along these bleak lines there is a haunting story told by Elie Wiesel in his book *Night*, which is an account of his experiences in the Nazi concentration camps at Buchenwald and Auschwitz. He recalls an unbearable day when the camp inmates were forced by the SS to watch a public hanging of three prisoners, two adults and a young boy, whom he refers to as "the sad-eyed angel":

> Three victims in chains—and one of them, the little servant, the sad-eyed angel. . . . The three necks were placed at the same moment within the nooses. . . . "Where is God? Where is He?" someone behind me asked. At a sign from the head of the camp, the three chairs tipped over. Total silence throughout the camp. On the horizon, the sun was setting. "Bare your heads!" yelled the head of the camp. His voice was raucous. We were weeping. "Cover your heads!"
>
> Then the march past began. The two adults were no longer alive. Their tongues hung swollen, blue-tinged. But the third rope was still moving; being so light, the child was still alive. For more than half an hour he stayed there, struggling between life and death, dying in slow agony under our eyes. And we had to look him full in the face. He was still alive when I passed in front of him. His tongue was still red, his eyes were not yet glazed.
>
> Behind me, I heard the same man asking: "Where is God now?" And I heard a voice within me answer him: "Where is He? Here He is—He is hanging here on this gallows."[39]

Wiesel does not offer a theological explanation. Does a shatter-ing experience like this destroy one's faith in God? Or one's faith in human decency, goodness, justice, mercy? Is the torture and killing of the innocent—the sad-eyed angel and millions of oth-ers—equivalent to the torture and killing of God? Is the demonic cruelty of the Holocaust the ultimate proof that God is *dead*? Or *useless*? Or *mean*? All honest questions. Witnesses and survivors have the right to ask them all.

Elizabeth Johnson offers some sobering thoughts on Wiesel's story in her book *Quest for the Living God*. She believes the "Where is God?" question is the most appropriate and promising place to begin in the face of such atrocity and evil. Otherwise, we get lost in impossible questions like *why* God could let this happen; or *how* a loving God could allow this to happen with-out intervening on behalf of the victims; or even, perhaps, how could God *do* such a thing? "The proper question," says Johnson, "is not *why* did God permit this to happen, or *how* this can be reconciled with divine governance of the world. Rather . . . the proper question becomes the anguished query: *where* is God, where is God now?"[40]

The answer Wiesel heard within himself was, "He is hanging here on this gallows." It would be arrogant and presumptuous to impose a Christian interpretation on his inner voice, to co-opt the suffer-ing of Jewish people with Christian language, particularly because the monstrous crimes of the Holocaust were largely perpetrated by so-called Christians. Still, it is hard not to think of the sad-eyed angel as yet another embodiment of the crucified God, a helpless God who is desecrated *whenever* and *wherever* innocent human be-ings are desecrated.

Not so implicit in this kind of thinking is the idea that God is not neutral about the plight of the innocent. Dorothee Soelle, a German theologian whose thinking was profoundly influenced by the massive historical trauma of the Holocaust, offers her own thoughts on Wiesel's story:

The decisive phrase, that God is hanging "here on this gallows" has two meanings. First, it is an assertion about God.
God is no executioner—and no almighty spectator (which
would amount to the same thing). Between the sufferer and
the one who causes the suffering, between the victim and the
executioner, God, whatever people make of this word, is on
the side of the sufferer. God is on the side of the victim. He
is hanged.[41]

God takes sides. God suffers with. "The mystery of God emerges
even more clearly in this world of victims," writes Sobrino, "for
this is a God who not only favors the victims but is at the mercy
of their torturers."[42]

I am thinking of a torture survivor, Matilde de la Sierra, who
wrestled deeply with these questions for many years, and who
eventually reached similar conclusions.

Matilde grew up in Guatemala City. Her father, Arnaldo, was a
doctor, and her mother, Victoria, was a nurse. The violence of the
thirty-six-year Guatemalan civil war was the background of her
childhood, although it mainly took place at some remove from
the capital in the rural, highland areas of the country. Before it was
finally over in 1996, at least 150,000 would be killed (the great majority of whom were poor Mayan people murdered by government
forces), and 50,000 would be "disappeared," never to be seen again
by their families and loved ones.[43] In the Guatemalan context, to
"be disappeared" was to be kidnapped by military or intelligence
forces. This was usually followed by torture; some were tortured to
death, others killed after their torture. The bodies of *desaparecidos*
were disposed of in clandestine graves, garbage dumps, and various
other undignified places.

As the violence mounted in the early 1980s, Matilde's father continued his regular medical practice at a small clinic in the capital; he
also traveled regularly to a poor community outside the city where
he cared for anyone who needed help, including the occasional

guerrilla fighter from the armed resistance who might come for treatment. Because of this, it is believed that Arnaldo's name was added to a black list of "subversives." In 1981, he was abducted from in front of his clinic in Guatemala City, taken away in a van, and never seen again. He became yet another of the *desaparecidos* whose families would never have closure for their grief, and who would remain perpetually uncertain about the well-being and whereabouts of their loved ones.

Following the traumatic loss of her father, Matilde decided to emulate him by becoming a doctor herself. She remembers wishing and hoping and praying that her father would one day return, safe and sound, to attend her graduation from medical school. But when the day finally came, he didn't appear. Matilde later decided to live and work and care for the poor in a rural Mayan community in the northern highlands of Guatemala. Unfortunately, as turned out to be typical for those who cared for the poor in her country (doctors, priests, catechists, lawyers, and so on), she began to receive ominous, threatening letters. Finally, one night she was abducted by soldiers and taken to a clandestine place, where she was tortured and raped. After her release she went into hiding; eventually she made the painful decision to leave her beloved family and homeland to go into exile in the United States.

Matilde suffered for years from the devastating impact of her torture and rape, which she likened to a kind of emotional or spiritual death in a poem in which she described herself as a "dead woman walking." When asked about how the experience of torture affected her relationship with God, she recounts a protracted inner struggle with agonizing questions about why and how such terrible things could happen to her, to her father, to her people. For a long time she wrestled with feelings of guilt and anger, sometimes wondering if she deserved to be punished, other times challenging and confronting God for his seemingly harsh and cruel treatment of people like her who had tried to *be* good and *do* good. "How could you do this to me?" she protested. "Didn't I try to take care of your people?" Later, she shifted to questioning God's character: "How could you just stand by and let this happen to me?"

Finally, after some years, with the help of her therapist and a gifted spiritual director, Matilde began to come to a new realization about where God was when she was being tortured. "It wasn't that God was punishing me, or that God wasn't there, or that God didn't care. No, Jesus was right there with me. Jesus was being tortured too."

2

THE SCANDAL OF TORTURE

Outrages upon Human Dignity

To whom shall I speak and give warning,
    that they may hear?
See, their ears are closed,
    they cannot listen. . . .
They have treated the wound of my people carelessly,
    saying, "Peace, peace"
when there is no peace.
They acted shamefully, they committed abomination;
    yet they were not ashamed.
They did not know how to blush.
            —Jeremiah 6:10, 14–15

*Sometimes I think that's the trouble with the world: too many
people in high places who are stone-cold dead.*
            —Kurt Vonnegut[1]

NOT LONG AFTER the Abu Ghraib scandal broke in May 2004,
a reporter from the *Chicago Tribune* visited the Kovler Center to
interview a diverse group of torture survivors about their reactions to the lurid photos of tormented Iraqi prisoners.[2] All said

17

the images had triggered nightmarish personal memories of their own torture, sometimes including terrifying flashbacks in which they found themselves not only remembering but *reliving* their traumatic experiences. Some entered an exhausting period of sleepless nights and suffered demoralizing setbacks in their own recovery. Some survivors also reported that their faith in America had been shaken—especially their belief that their adopted country was a safe refuge from the horrors of torture. "I always wanted America to be morally super," said one man, "not just a superpower."[3] His feelings echo the profound sense of letdown felt by many Americans today.

This chapter begins with an exploration of the nature and scope of torture. What constitutes torture? What is the connection between torture and interrogation? Why are people tortured? What are some of the situational and systemic pressures that can make ordinary people engage in such extraordinarily cruel behavior? Along the way, I offer some thoughts on the practice of torture by my own country, the United States, which clandestinely dabbled in torture for many decades, but which began to practice torture more openly and shamelessly in the years after 9/11.

THE NATURE AND SCOPE OF TORTURE

What is torture? The United Nations Convention Against Torture and Other Cruel, Inhuman, or Degrading Treatment, adopted in 1984, offers this definition:

> Torture means any act by which severe pain or suffering, whether physical or mental, is intentionally inflicted by or at the instigation of a public official on a person for such purposes as obtaining from him or a third person information or confession, punishing him for an act he or a third person has committed or is suspected of having committed, or intimidating or coercing him or a third person, or for any reason based on discrimination of any kind, when such pain or suffering

is inflicted by or at the instigation of or with the consent or acquiescence of a public official or other person acting in an official capacity. (Art. 2)

A common justification for torture is the need to obtain information or confession, and so torture usually (though not always) occurs in conjunction with interrogation. *We have ways of making you talk.* Elaine Scarry examines the torture–interrogation link in her classic book *The Body in Pain*:

> Torture consists of a primary physical act, the infliction of pain, and a primary verbal act, the interrogation. The verbal act, in turn, consists of two parts, "the question" and "the answer." The first rarely occurs without the second. As is true of the present period, most historical episodes of torture, such as the Inquisition, have inevitably included the element of interrogation: the pain is accompanied by "the Question."[4]

Questions abound about the reliability and validity of answers given to interrogators by persons under torture. Ulpian, a third-century Roman jurist, described torture *(quaestio)* as "the torment and suffering of the body in order to elicit the truth."[5] Although torture can indeed be an effective means of coercing some people to give up "the truth," what if a person doesn't *know* "the truth"? What if he or she is not in possession of the desired information and is therefore unable to provide the answers sought by the interrogator? Frantz Fanon puts it very simply: "There are two types of people who are tortured: 1) Those who know something. 2) Those who know nothing."[6] Is the "I don't know!" of the tortured person to be accepted at face value by the interrogator? Or is it likely to be interpreted as evasiveness or willful withholding of information, perhaps justifying continuation or even escalation of the torture?

There is also the problem of torture generating "false positive" information from people who may, in desperation, say *anything* to get their torments to stop. A striking example is Khalid Sheikh Mohammed, the alleged planner of the 9/11 attacks, who is known to have been waterboarded 183 times by the Central Intelligence Agency (CIA) in March 2003. In an interview with representatives of the International Committee of the Red Cross (ICRC), he explained:

> During the harshest period of my interrogation I gave a lot of false information in order to satisfy what I believed the interrogators wished to hear in order to make the ill-treatment stop. I later told the interrogators that their methods were stupid and counterproductive. I'm sure that the false information I was forced to invent in order to make the ill-treatment stop wasted a lot of their time and led to several false red-alerts being placed in the US.[7]

Sometimes false information generated by torture can have disastrous consequences. A tragic example is the case of Ibn al-Shaik al-Libi, a former "high-value detainee" who invented a false story under torture that Saddam Hussein had trained Al Qaeda operatives in the use of biological and chemical weapons. Although intelligence personnel had serious doubts about al-Libi's credibility, the story was later cited by the Bush administration as part of its justification to launch the Iraq war—most famously by Secretary of State Colin Powell at the United Nations in February 2003.

Al-Libi, who was captured in Afghanistan in late 2001, vanished into the secret "black site" detention system run by the CIA and was eventually transferred to the custody of Egyptian intelligence for further interrogation and torture. After being beaten and subjected to a "mock burial" by being placed for seventeen hours in a cramped box, al-Libi made up the story about the Iraq–Al Qaeda connection to get the Egyptians to stop torturing him. He later recanted the story when he was returned to the custody of the CIA, but only after it had been used to shore up the shaky case of an administration hellbent on war. Rather than being sent to Guantanamo with other high-value detainees in 2006, al-Libi became a "ghost prisoner" whose whereabouts were only discovered in April 2009, just a few weeks before he died of an apparent suicide in a Libyan prison.[8] "I would speculate that he was missing because he was such an embarrassment to the Bush administration," said Tom Malinowski, head of the Washington office of Human Rights Watch. "He was Exhibit A in the narrative that tortured confessions contributed to the massive intelligence failure that preceded the Iraq war."[9]

The surface rationale of obtaining information through torture may also mask other underlying motives to mistreat prisoners, such as stifling dissent, intimidation of opposition, individual punishment, or collective punishment of whole communities. Some people are released after torture with the intent of sending a terrifying message to their communities by way of the psychological and physical trauma of the survivor.

Interrogators can also be motivated by sadistic or vindictive inclinations that have nothing to do with obtaining information. The slogans of South Vietnamese torturers of suspected members of the Viet Cong provide a crude example: "If they are not guilty, beat them until they are," or, "If you are not a Viet Cong, we will beat you until you admit you are; and if you admit you are, we will beat you until you no longer dare to be one."[10] Answers to "the Question" may be irrelevant, as evident in the following account of Dianna Ortiz, an American missionary sister who was brutally tortured by Guatemalan intelligence personnel in 1989:

> They've taken my sweatshirt off and are explaining the rules. "We're going to ask you some questions. If you give an answer we like, we'll let you smoke. If we don't like the answer, we'll burn you." "The rules are unfair," I venture. They burn me. They ask me my name, age, and place of residence. The anticipation is worse than the burns—wondering if this answer

is good enough. But for every answer I give, they burn me. Every time I am silent they burn me. My throat becomes raw from screaming.[11]

Days after she managed to escape, a doctor would find more than 111 cigarette burns on her back alone. In addition to the burns and other horrors, Ortiz was also gang-raped by her torturers.

Many are killed when their torturers are finished with them, either because they are no longer considered useful or to cover up evidence of depraved, criminal behavior. Still others are tortured to death through excesses of cruelty—some deliberately, others inadvertently. This was the case with two prisoners, Habibullah and Dilawar, who were tortured to death by US personnel at the Bagram Collection Point detention center in Afghanistan in December 2002.[12]

Habibullah, an intense, forty-two-year-old Afghan man admitted to the Bagram facility on November 30, 2002, was hooded and kept in a standing position with his wrists shackled to the ceiling of his cell for the greater part of the final four days of his life. The shackling was a standard procedure for the first twenty-four to seventy-two hours of detention at Bagram. It was used primarily for the purpose of sleep deprivation; each time the prisoner fell asleep, he would awaken from the pain of the full weight of his body hanging from his wrists. (In the Middle Ages torture by sleep deprivation was known as *tormentum insomniae.*)

Habibullah developed a reputation for being uncooperative and insubordinate after he became combative during a rectal exam soon after his arrival at Bagram. He also talked back when he was being abused. Guards and military police had been trained in an approved technique known as the *common peroneal strike,* which involved the delivery of a sharp, potentially disabling blow (usually with a knee or kick) to the side of the leg, just above the knee. Habibullah was regularly punished with peroneal strikes as he hung in chains from the ceiling—to the point that he was unable to bend his knees and could hardly stand or walk. He was unshackled from the ceiling only for interrogation sessions, during which he was verbally abused and physically assaulted. By December 2, he was coughing up phlegm and complaining of chest pains. On December 3, after four days of mounting agony from this treatment, he was found dead, hanging limply from his chains. An autopsy showed evidence of deep contusions on his thighs, knees, and calves. The Army coroner, who ruled the death a homicide, attributed his death to a blood clot from the severe injuries to his legs that had traveled to his heart and blocked the flow of blood to his lungs.[13]

Dilawar, a slight, shy, twenty-two-year-old Afghan farmer and part-time taxi driver, was delivered into the custody of US forces at Bagram the day after Habibullah's death.[14] He was apprehended because he happened to drive his taxi past an American base with three male passengers on the same day the base had been attacked by rocket fire. The three passengers were shipped off to the US prison at Guantanamo Bay but were released fifteen months later without charges. Dilawar remained at Bagram.

Although there is evidence from later testimony that some interrogators believed Dilawar to be an innocent man who had been in the wrong place at the wrong time, he was nonetheless subjected to the brutal Bagram routine of hooding, shackling in a standing position, brutal peroneal strikes to his legs, and harsh, physically assaultive interrogation sessions. At one point interrogators tried to force him to his knees, but he was unable to kneel because his legs were so damaged from the leg strikes. At another, interrogators repeatedly attempted to force him to stand against the wall, but he kept sliding down because he was unable to stand. Hanging in shackles in his cell, Dilawar was heard crying over and over again for his mother and father. Some soldiers began using peroneal strikes to "shut him up" because he was yelling and screaming so much. It became a running joke to deliver a strike just to hear him scream, "Allah! Allah! Allah!" Over one hundred peroneal strikes were delivered during one twenty-four-hour period. He was heard rambling incoherently, talking about how his young wife had come to visit him in his cell. Five days after his arrival at Bagram, Dilawar was dead, swaying in his shackles. The Army coroner, Lt. Col. Elizabeth Rouse, listed the cause of death as heart failure caused by "blunt force injuries to the lower extremities." His legs had "basically been pulpified," she later testified. "I've seen similar injuries in an individual run over by a bus."[15]

Even after the coroner ruled the deaths of Dilawar and Habibullah homicides, General Daniel McNeil, then commander of US forces in Afghanistan, publicly maintained in February 2003 that both men had died of "natural causes."[16] Although an Army criminal inquiry was begun into the deaths of the two men, it moved very slowly. In the meantime Captain Carolyn Wood, the chief operations officer of the Bagram interrogators, was redeployed to Iraq and in July 2003 took charge of interrogations at Abu Ghraib prison. By October 2004, the Army's Criminal Investigation Command had concluded that there was probable cause to charge twenty-seven officers and enlisted personnel with criminal offenses in the Dilawar case (with fifteen of the same soldiers cited in the Habibullah case); charges ranged from dereliction of duty to maiming to involuntary manslaughter. Of these, only a few lower-level soldiers were convicted; most were acquitted or received light sentences (two to five months in military prison), reprimands, or reductions in rank.

Even though it was obvious that Habibullah and Dilawar died as a result of, in the words of the UN Convention Against Torture, "suffering inflicted by or at the instigation of or with the consent or acquiescence of a public official or other person acting in an official capacity," no higher-ranking military officers or government officials were ever found criminally responsible for their deaths. Army Colonel Lawrence Wilkerson believed otherwise and believed that such responsibility existed. As Chief of Staff to Secretary of State Colin Powell from 2002 to 2005, Wilkerson expressed concern that intense pressures on lower-level soldiers to produce intelligence, along with encouragement from superiors to "take the gloves off" in their treatment of detainees, were coming from the highest levels of the White House and the Pentagon.[17] This included directives from President Bush and Secretary of Defense Rumsfeld that the Geneva Conventions did not apply to treatment of detainees in the "War on Terror." "I was developing the picture as to how this all got started in the first place," said Wilkerson, "and that alarmed me as much as the abuse itself because it looked like authorization for the abuse went to the very top of the United States government."[18]

THE UNITED STATES AND THE DARK SIDE

Since the 9/11 attacks, there has been a marked erosion of respect for human rights at the highest levels of the US government, military, and intelligence establishments. This wickedness in high places has trickled down, resulting in a loss of moral bearings in the wider culture. Public discourse has moved from regard for torture as an aberrant and barbaric practice to an open debate about the circumstances under which it is permissible. Polls suggest that a large percentage of Americans now believe that torture is justified, at least in certain situations, to prevent terrorism and to protect "national security."[19]

In American popular culture the shift can be seen in television series and movies in the post-9/11 period. An example is the hit television series "24," which ran for eight seasons from 2001 to 2010. The main character, Jack Bauer, is a heroic counterterrorism agent who routinely tortures terrorists—always under a "ticking time bomb" scenario—to get urgently needed information to prevent spectacular terrorist attacks. Another example is the controversial 2012 movie "Zero Dark Thirty," which graphically portrays scenes of torture and which gives the impression (accurate or not) that crucial information leading to finding Osama bin Laden was obtained through torture.

At a press conference on September 15, 2006, President George W. Bush gave the following response to a question about ongoing reports of maltreatment of prisoners in the custody of US military and intelligence services at places like Guantanamo Bay in Cuba, Abu Ghraib in Iraq, and Bagram in Afghanistan:

> This debate is occurring because the Supreme Court ruling said that we must conduct ourselves under the Common Article 3 of the Geneva Convention. And that Common Article 3 says that—you know—there will be no outrages on human dignity. It's like—it's very *vague*. What does that mean, "outrages upon human dignity"? That's a statement that's wide open to interpretation.

Bush was referring to the June 29, 2006, decision by the United States Supreme Court that all prisoners in US custody (including the CIA) must be treated in a manner consistent with the 1949 Geneva Conventions, including Common Article 3, which states, "The following acts are and shall remain prohibited at any time and in any place whatsoever: (a) violence to life and person, in particular murder of all kinds, mutilation, cruel treatment, and torture; (b) taking of hostages; (c) outrages upon personal dignity; in particular humiliating and degrading treatment."

A story comes to mind about the time a reporter asked Louis Armstrong the question, "Mr. Armstrong, what is jazz?" His response, "Man, if you gotta ask, you'll never know!" The same applies, I suppose, for a president who is unsure of the meaning of "outrages upon human dignity." A line from Graham Greene also seems apt: "In every government, there grows up a hideous Establishment of stupid men."[20]

Eyewitness accounts and testimonies about the maltreatment of prisoners during the Bush administration leave no doubt whatsoever about the kinds of things that constitute "outrages upon human dignity." For example, over three months after the Abu Ghraib photos were made public, an FBI counterterrorism official offered this account of what he observed during an August 2004 visit to the Guantanamo Bay prison:

> On a couple of occasions, I entered interview rooms to find a detainee chained hand and foot in a fetal position on the floor, with no chair, food, or water. Most times they had urinated or defecated on themselves, and had been left there for 18 to 24 hours or more. . . . When I asked the M.P.s what was going on, I was told that the interrogators from the day before had ordered this treatment, and the detainee was not to be moved. On another occasion . . . the detainee was almost unconscious on the floor, with a pile of hair next to him. He had apparently been literally pulling his own hair out through the night.[21]

The Guantanamo Bay prison was established through the chicanery of the Bush administration as a weird, extralegal, offshore anomaly that would make it possible for the rights of prisoners to be routinely violated beyond the reach of annoying and inconvenient legal and humanitarian scrutiny. The first twenty prisoners arrived in shackles and orange jumpsuits on January 11, 2002, accompanied by an announcement from President Bush that they would *not* be entitled to the protections of the Geneva Conventions. Since then, a total of 774 prisoners have been held at the facility for varying lengths of time. Although Secretary of Defense Donald Rumsfeld referred to the Guantanamo inmates as the "worst of the worst," over 600 were subsequently released without charges or transferred to other countries. It is known that the great majority were either innocent or held on evidence that was unlikely to hold up in a court of law—either because it was flimsy to begin with, or because it was obtained through torture.[22]

The Bush administration also devised another secret program, administered by the CIA, under which certain suspected terrorists could be detained and interrogated, according to President Bush, in "an environment where they can be held secretly [and] questioned by experts" using "an alternative set of procedures."[23] These clandestine CIA prisons (located in countries that included Egypt, Syria, Thailand, Libya, Poland, and Morocco) came to be known as "black sites." Beyond strictest secrecy, this designation is also suggestive of the kinds of dark activities that are known to have occurred in these places, which gave evidence that the United States had indeed crossed over to what Vice President Dick Cheney had referred to as "the Dark Side." In an appearance on *Meet the Press* on September 16, 2001, the first Sunday after 9/11, Cheney offered these ominous comments:

> We'll have to work, sort of, the Dark Side, if you will. We've got to spend time in the shadows of the intelligence world. A lot of what needs to be done here will have to be done quietly, without any discussion, using sources and methods that are available to our intelligence agencies—if we are going to be successful. That's the world these folks operate in. And, uh, so it's going to be vital for us to use any means at our disposal, basically, to achieve our objectives.[24]

Interrogation and torture were also "outsourced" by the CIA through the illegal and oddly named "extraordinary rendition" program, whereby as many as 150 prisoners were transferred to other countries to be interrogated and tortured by foreign surrogates who forwarded any information obtained (true or false) to the CIA.[25] President Bush announced in September 2006 that fourteen of these "high value detainees" who had previously been held by the CIA in either black sites or the rendition program would be transferred to Guantanamo Bay. Shortly after their arrival the ICRC, the body charged with overseeing compliance with the Geneva Conventions, was allowed to interview these prisoners. In February 2007 the "ICRC Report on the Treatment of Fourteen

'High-Value Detainees' in CIA Custody" was forwarded to the US government. The report pointedly concluded:

> The allegations of ill-treatment of the detainees indicate that, in many cases, the ill-treatment to which they were subjected while held in the CIA program, either singly or in combination, constituted torture. In addition, many other elements of the ill-treatment, either singly or in combination, constituted cruel, inhuman, or degrading treatment.[26]

Since all of these detainees had been held in continuous solitary confinement and "incommunicado detention" since their capture, and had therefore had no opportunities to communicate or compare notes with one another, the similarity and consistency of their stories of maltreatment were striking. The twelve most common techniques of ill-treatment described by the prisoners are codified in the ICRC report as follows:

- *Suffocation by water* poured over a cloth placed over the nose and mouth, alleged by three of the fourteen.
- *Prolonged stress standing position,* naked, held with the arms extended and chained above the head, as alleged by ten of the fourteen, for periods from two or three days continuously, and for up to two or three months intermittently, during which period toilet access was sometimes denied resulting in allegations from four detainees that they had to defecate and urinate over themselves [some were made to wear diapers].
- *Beatings by use of a collar* held around the detainee's neck and used to forcefully bang the head and body against the wall, alleged by six of the fourteen.
- *Beating and kicking,* including slapping, punching, kicking to the body and face, alleged by nine of the fourteen.

- *Confinement in a box* to severely restrict movement alleged in the case of one detainee.
- *Prolonged nudity* alleged by eleven of the fourteen during detention, interrogation and ill-treatment; this enforced nudity lasted for periods ranging from several weeks to several months.
- *Sleep deprivation* was alleged by eleven of the fourteen through days of interrogation, through use of forced stress positions (standing or sitting), cold water and use of repetitive loud noise or music. One detainee was kept sitting on a chair for prolonged periods of time.
- *Exposure to cold temperature* was alleged by most of the fourteen, especially via cold cells and interrogation rooms, and for seven of them, by the use of cold water poured over the body or, as alleged by three of the detainees, held around the body by means of a plastic sheet to create an immersion bath with just the head out of the water.
- *Prolonged shackling* of hands and/or feet was alleged by many of the fourteen.
- *Threats of ill-treatment* to the detainee and/or his family, alleged by nine of the fourteen.
- *Forced shaving of the head and beard,* alleged by two of the fourteen.
- *Deprivation/restricted provision of solid food* from 3 days to 1 month after arrest, alleged by eight of the fourteen.[27]

The first technique, *suffocation by water,* is more commonly known as waterboarding. Although it can take various perverse forms, it basically involves a kind of controlled near-drowning; survival depends upon the timing and judgment of the torturers to stop before the prisoner actually drowns. This induces absolute terror and panic in the tortured persons as they begin to drown and die.

The CIA has admitted that three detainees were waterboarded prior to their transfer to Guantanamo, including Khalid Sheikh Mohammed (the alleged planner of the 9/11 attacks), Abu Zubayda (an alleged Al Qaeda operative), and Abd al-Rashim al-Nashiri (another alleged Al Qaeda operative). In addition to being waterboarded twice, al-Nashiri was also subjected to other unorthodox "alternative procedures," including holding a handgun to his head and revving a power drill as he stood hooded and naked. He also alleged that he was threatened with sodomy and with the arrest and rape of his family.

Waterboarding was used a total of 266 times on two particular suspects, Khalid Sheik Mohammed and Abu Zubayda. Mohammed was waterboarded 183 times during March 2003, and Zubayda was waterboarded 83 times in August 2002.[28] Zubayda was also kept in a small cage, too small to stand upright, for long periods of time. He referred to the cage as a "dog box." This account of his waterboarding is found in the ICRC report:

> I was then dragged from the small box, unable to walk properly and put on what looked like a hospital bed, and strapped down very tightly with belts. A black cloth was then placed over my face and the interrogators used a mineral water bottle to pour water over the cloth so that I could not breathe. After a few minutes the cloth was removed and the bed was rotated into an upright position. The pressure of the straps on my wounds was very painful. I vomited. The bed was again lowered to horizontal position and the same torture carried out again with the black cloth over my face and water poured from a bottle. On this occasion my head was in a more backward, downwards position and the water was poured on for a longer time. I struggled against the straps, trying to breathe, but it was hopeless. I thought I was going to die. I lost control of my urine. Since then I still lose control of my urine when under stress.[29]

Although President Barack Obama signed an executive order on January 22, 2009, ordering that the Guantanamo Bay prison be closed within a year, it remains open five years later. His initial efforts were met with tremendous resistance from members of Congress who apparently did not wish to appear "soft" on terrorism. Obama's public statements reveal a certain embarrassment about Guantanamo and a preference to close the place, but he appears to have largely given up on trying to do so and has even embraced the system of indefinite detention and unfair trials—really *no* trials—that it was founded upon.[30] Further, rather than dealing with inconvenient diplomatic and logistical and legal hassles associated with capturing and legally prosecuting suspected terrorists, he has markedly expanded the program of targeted assassination of them by missiles fired from unmanned aerial drones. In the interests of national security Obama rationalizes the extrajudicial killing of suspected enemies—and any other man, woman, or child who is unfortunate enough to be within range of the blast—in countries with whom we are not at war, including Pakistan, Yemen, and Somalia.[31]

As of August 2013, 166 men remain at Guantanamo. Of these, 157 have not been charged with a crime; 87 have been cleared for release but nonetheless remain imprisoned. As I write, over 100 inmates are on a hunger strike to protest their unjust imprisonment.[32] Over 40 are being force-fed with nasal gastric feeding tubes—a clear violation of medical ethics with persons who are competent to make their own decisions, and which itself is a form of inhumane and degrading treatment that is tantamount to torture.[33] In an April 14, 2013, *New York Times* editorial titled "Gitmo Is Killing Me," one hunger striker, a Yemeni citizen named Samir Naji al Hasan Moqbel, appealed for the world to take notice:

> I've been on hunger strike since February 10 and have lost well over 30 pounds. I will not eat until they restore my dignity. I have been detained at Guantanamo for 11 years and three months. I have never been charged with any crime. I have

never received a trial. I could have been home years ago—no one seriously thinks I am a threat—but I am still here. . . . The only reason I am still here is that President Obama refuses to send any detainees back to Yemen. This makes no sense. I am a human being, not a passport, and I deserve to be treated like one. . . . The situation is desperate now. All of the detainees here are suffering deeply. . . . I just hope that because of the pain we are suffering, the eyes of the world will once again look to Guantanamo before it is too late.

Another Yemeni prisoner, Adnan Farhan Abdul Latif, had been recommended for release by the Department of Defense in 2006, 2008, and 2009, and a US district court judge ruled in 2010 that his detention was unlawful because of the government's lack of evidence. Latif died in solitary confinement at age thirty-six on September 8, 2012, after languishing at Guantanamo for nearly eleven years.[34] His death was later reported as a suicide resulting from an overdose of psychiatric medication, but questions remain about how a prisoner could manage to collect enough medication to kill himself in such a strictly monitored prison environment.[35] Latif was eventually returned to his homeland in a body bag. Guantanamo remains a global symbol of injustice and cruelty.

CONDITIONS OF ATROCITY

How can anybody do this to another human being? This was the question that haunted a young Irishman named Jim Auld as he was being tortured in a British prison in Northern Ireland. As violence escalated against the British occupation forces in the early 1970s, hundreds of young Irish men and women were detained, interrogated, and tortured by British military intelligence to see what they knew about the activities of the resurgent Irish Republican Army movement. Among them was Auld, a twenty-year-old unemployed dental technician who was "lifted" in a British Army sweep of a

Catholic neighborhood in Belfast one night in 1971. Along with the standard vicious beatings, he was brutally tortured with what came to be known as the five techniques: hooding, noise bombardment, sleep deprivation, food deprivation, and wall standing. After being held without charge or trial for over a year, Auld was released, in a psychotic state, to a psychiatric institution.

Jim Auld's story is one of many in John Conroy's *Unspeakable Acts, Ordinary People,* which is based on personal interviews with victims and perpetrators of torture in three very different locales: Irish Catholics in British prisons in Northern Ireland during "the Troubles"; Palestinians from the West Bank under interrogation by Israeli Army and Israeli Intelligence personnel in the late 1980s; and African American criminal suspects in the custody of the Chicago police between 1972 and 1991.[36] Among other things, the book examines the question of how ordinary people can engage in extraordinarily cruel behavior toward other human beings.

A partial answer is that some people are "bad apples" who are predisposed to aggressive, violent, dishonest, or cruel behavior. Because of their troubled personal histories or personality structure, they lack a sense of empathy—a capacity for genuine concern and feeling for the pain of others. They also lack a sense of conscience—a capacity to feel appropriate guilt and remorse when they have hurt or violated the rights of others. Historically, psychiatry has variously described such persons as psychopaths or sociopaths; in the last few decades they have been categorized by the diagnostic label of antisocial personality disorder. It is not surprising that a certain number of such disturbed people find their way into military or intelligence or police services, where they can do great harm—especially when they are in positions of power or authority over people in their custody or control.

But the great majority of people who engage in torture or wartime atrocities are not psychopathic monsters. "Monsters exist," wrote Primo Levi in his chilling reflections on the sadism of some Nazi commandants and guards at the concentration camps, "but they are too few in number to be really dangerous. More dangerous are the common men, the functionaries ready to believe and act without asking questions."[37] For the purposes of this book, I am less interested in the monsters or "bad apples" and more concerned with understanding the kinds of systemic pressures and forces that can make the "functionaries" behave badly.

Blaming a few deviant, low-level soldiers for a scandal like Abu Ghraib not only deflects attention away from those who hold command responsibility for such atrocities, but also serves a wider defensive purpose of protecting the rest of us from the humbling recognition that the torturers, after all, are not all that different from us. Psychoanalyst Neil Altman is clear on this:

> When torture is publicly shown to have taken place, per-
> petrated by US agents, those involved are portrayed by the
> government and in the media as deviant individuals, rather
> than as people who were swept up in a dynamic, emotional
> process that any and all of us would have been powerfully sub-
> ject to under certain conditions. We maintain the fiction that
> the problem is a few "bad apples," thus aborting the process
> of reflecting on the disease of which those individuals are but
> symptoms, a disease to which all of us are vulnerable.[38]

The culture of obedience in military and prison situations certainly plays a significant role in the turning of basically good people
toward evil. Those that Primo Levi refers to as "functionaries" do
what they are *told* to do—either out of a wish to please authorities
or fear of the consequences if they don't comply. "I was just following orders" becomes the excuse for unjust or inhumane behavior;
this has been known as the "Nuremberg defense" ever since the
trials of the Nazi war criminals.

The widely known psychological experiments of Stanley Milgram, in which participants were instructed to administer what they
thought was a real electric shock to a human subject, demonstrated

how people can be capable of inflicting pain on others simply because they are asked to do so by an authority figure—even when
it violates their own conscience. In "The Perils of Obedience"
Milgram writes:

> This is, perhaps, the most fundamental lesson of our study:
> Ordinary people, simply doing their jobs, and without any
> particular hostility on their part, can become agents in a ter-
> rible destructive process. Moreover, even when the destructive
> effects of their work become patently clear, and they are asked
> to carry out actions incompatible with fundamental standards
> of morality, relatively few people have the resources needed
> to resist authority.[39]

Private Damien Corsetti, who served as an interrogator in the US
519th Military Intelligence Unit at both Bagram and Abu Ghraib
prisons, was nicknamed "King of Torture" and "Monster" by his fellow soldiers.[40] (He actually had the Italian word for monster, *mostro*,
tattooed on his stomach.) In the investigation into criminal abuses
of prisoners at Bagram prison, Corsetti was charged with dereliction
of duty, maltreatment, assault, and performing an indecent act with
another person (he was later cleared of all charges). At his court
martial a detainee who claimed to have been abused by Corsetti
was able to describe the monster tattoo in detail.

Although it might be tempting to conclude that Damien Corsetti's tattoo is a sign of deeper underlying psychopathology, it would
be unfair to do so based only on secondhand reports. It is probably
safe to assume, however, that Corsetti was one among many young
soldiers who found themselves caught up in the destructive insanity
of the early phases of the so-called War on Terror. There are dynamics in certain situations that can bring out the worst in people. In
Corsetti's own words: "You put people in a crazy situation and people
do crazy things."[41] Robert Jay Lifton has referred to such crazy-
making circumstances as "atrocity-producing situations," which he

defines as being "so structured, psychologically and militarily, that ordinary people, men or women no better or worse than you or I, can regularly commit atrocities."[42]

In a May 2004 editorial written in response to the Abu Ghraib scandal, Philip Zimbardo writes: "Human behavior is much more under the control of situational forces than most of us recognize or want to acknowledge. In a situation that implicitly gives permission for suspending moral values, many of us can be morphed into creatures alien to our usual natures."[43] Zimbardo is the psychologist known for the controversial Stanford prison experiment, in which college student participants were assigned roles as guards and prisoners in a mock prison environment. When some of the guards began to behave in authoritarian and even sadistic ways, and when some of the prisoners began to show marked signs of emotional distress and trauma, it became necessary to terminate the two-week experiment after only six days. The experiment has stimulated decades of reflection on the kinds of systemic dynamics and pressures that can lead to abuses of power in prison environments. Zimbardo was especially struck by the parallels between the photos of real guards tormenting real prisoners at Abu Ghraib and the dynamics he had observed between role-playing guards and prisoners in his experiment. This was the inspiration for his book, *The Lucifer Effect: Understanding How Good People Turn Evil.*[44]

In his reflections on parallels between atrocities committed by US soldiers during the Vietnam war and more recent war crimes in Afghanistan and Iraq, Lifton has identified some of the common features of such situations:

> Iraq is also a counterinsurgency war in which US soldiers, despite their extraordinary firepower, feel extremely vulnerable in a hostile environment, and in which higher-ranking officers and war planners feel frustrated by the great difficulty of tracking down or even recognizing the enemy. The exaggerated focus on interrogation, including the humiliation of

detainees as a "softening-up" process, reflects that frustration.[45]

In his analysis of the Abu Ghraib scandal, Lifton suggests that a "three-tier" dynamic was operative. On the bottom tier were prison personnel, including the foot soldiers (military police, civilian contractors, and guards) and the military intelligence officers in charge of interrogations at the prison. The foot soldiers did the "dirty work" under the direction of the intelligence officers, who were acting under pressure from the second tier of higher-up officers in Iraq to extract information that might help to identify "insurgents" and hidden weaponry. Anxieties and pressures increased as US casualties mounted in the bloody mayhem that was set in motion by the invasion and occupation. Ultimately, it was top-down pressures from the third tier—the highest levels of the US government and military—that were driving the whole thing:

> What ultimately drives the dynamic is an ideological vision that equates Iraqi prisoners with "terrorists" and seeks to further justify the invasion. All this is part of the amorphous, even apocalyptic, "war on terrorism," as is the practice of denying the human rights of detainees labeled as terrorists, a further stimulus for abuse. . . . To attribute the Abu Ghraib scandal to "a few bad apples" or to "individual failures" is poor psychology and self-serving pseudomorality. To be sure individual soldiers and civilians who participated in it are accountable for their behavior, even under pressured conditions. But the greater responsibility lies with those who planned and executed the war on Iraq and the "war on terrorism" of which it is a part, and who created, in policy and attitude, the accompanying denial of rights of captives and suspects. Psychologically and ethically, responsibility for the crimes at Abu Ghraib extends to the Defense Secretary, the Attorney General, and the White House.[46]

Although there is overwhelming evidence in the public record of the connivance of Bush administration officials in the creation and promotion of an elaborate torture program, little or nothing has been done to hold the architects of this program accountable.[47] Although President Obama has spoken out against torture, he has also discouraged all efforts to investigate the crimes of the previous administration. "I'm a strong believer," he explained, "that it's important to look forward and not backward." The unfortunate result has been a climate of impunity for officials who remain unapologetic and unrepentant about their flagrant disregard for domestic and international law, and who, in some cases, have literally been allowed to get away with murder. Despite such efforts to forget and move on, the sin of torture will continue to haunt and undermine forward progress until it is sufficiently confronted. "Historical amnesia is a dangerous phenomenon," writes Noam Chomsky, "not only because it undermines moral and intellectual integrity, but also because it lays the groundwork for crimes that lie ahead."[48]

On an individual level many interrogators and guards are haunted for the rest of their lives by having participated in the torture of other human beings. "When you cross over that line of darkness," said one former CIA officer, "it's hard to come back. You lose your soul. You can do your best to justify it, but it's well outside the norm. You can't go to that dark a place without it changing you."[49] Some are emotionally and spiritually crippled by the violence that torture has done—not only to their victims, but to their own consciences. Too much rationalizing of evil behavior has desensitized them to normal human feelings of empathy and guilt. "Our torturers," wrote Aleksandr Solzhenitsyn, "have been punished most horribly of all: they are turning into swine, they are departing downward from humanity."[50] Others remain human—perhaps *because* they suffer from uneasy consciences and are tormented by persistent shame and guilt over what they have done. They suffer from what has been called "moral injury." Their inner pain is characterized by a complex mix of post-traumatic stress symptoms—which resemble the emotional suffering of their victims—but with an added burden of stinging guilt and shame for having been the perpetrator of such suffering.[51]

Torture is bad all around. It dehumanizes both its victims and its perpetrators, and it damages the moral fabric of societies that endorse or tolerate it. "The quickest way to lose your humanity," warned William Sloane Coffin, "is to begin to tolerate the intolerable."[52]

3

CRUCIFIED PEOPLES

Many Suffer So a Few May Enjoy

Ecce homo: behold the emaciated, tear-stained, terrified face of Christ, desecrated in the masses of the world's poor, the crucified peoples.
—Elizabeth Johnson[1]

The nobodies: nobody's children, owners of nothing. The nobodies: the no ones, the nobodied, running like rabbits, dying through life, screwed every which way.
—Eduardo Galeano[2]

IGNACIO ELLACURÍA REFERRED to the people nearest to his heart as *el pueblo crucificado*, "the crucified people." By this, in particular, he meant the poor of El Salvador, the country that had become his home. More broadly, though, he meant to include *all* people in the world whose lives are a life-and-death struggle with unjust poverty and oppression.[3] They are the ones Jesus referred to as "the least" and "the last." Frantz Fanon called them "the wretched of the earth."[4]

In this chapter I shift briefly away from the reality of actual torture to the use of crucifixion as an evocative metaphor to convey the collective suffering of entire human communities. I begin by exploring what Ellacuría means when he refers to certain peoples as crucified. Then I examine some historical and contemporary examples of crucified peoples, beginning with the impact of European colonialism on indigenous peoples in Latin America and Africa. Finally, there are the oppressive economic and systemic forces that *make* people poor and *keep* people poor—that put them on the cross and keep them hanging there.

THE LANGUAGE OF CRUCIFIXION

Ellacuría was one of six Jesuits who were murdered, along with their housekeeper and her daughter, by Salvadoran armed forces on the lawn outside the Jesuit residence at the University of Central America in San Salvador on the night of November 16, 1989.[5] Besides Ellacuría, the dead included Ignacio Martín-Baro, the Jesuit social psychologist whose work was the inspiration for the movement that has come to be known as liberation psychology.[6] The people of El Salvador, where these men lived and worked and died during the bloody passion of that tortured land, taught them deep lessons about the collective meanings of crucifixion, and about the personal sacrifices that might be necessary, in Ellacuría's words, to "take the crucified people from the cross."

Jon Sobrino, a member of the same community who escaped death only because he happened to be away at the time his Jesuit brothers were murdered, has said that crucifixion is really the only way adequately to convey the enormity and gravity of the actual situation of so many people in the world:

> *Crucified peoples* is useful and necessary language at the real level of fact, because cross means death. . . . It is slow but real death caused by the poverty generated by unjust structures. . . . It is swift, violent death, caused by repression and wars, when the poor threaten these unjust structures. To die crucified does

not mean simply to die, but to be put to death; it means there
are victims and there are executioners. . . . Crucified peoples
exist. It is necessary and urgent to see our world this way. And
it is right to call them this, because this language stresses their
historical tragedy and their meaning for faith.[7]

Crucified peoples include historically persecuted and oppressed
communities like the Jews of Europe, West Africans kidnapped for
slavery in the Americas (and their descendants), the indigenous
peoples of colonial Latin America and Africa and Asia (and their
postcolonial descendants), and the Native Americans of North
America. They include all those conquered and subjugated and
exploited by various empires through the ages—from the ancient
Romans, through the British and French and Spanish, and others,
all the way to more recent brutal manifestations of US imperialism
in Latin America and the Middle East. They also include excluded
and oppressed minorities within societies (for example, Palestinians
in Israel/Palestine, the Roma people of Europe, undocumented immigrants in the United States, African American and Latino youth
from the inner cities of the United States, and sexual minorities
pretty much everywhere).

Although many communities experience painful forms of discrimination and social exclusion, the focus here will be on those
who suffer in extreme forms of poverty and violent political repression. Also, though there are many degrees of poverty and many
kinds of need, the interest here will be in those who live most
precariously and miserably in extreme poverty (roughly defined as
those who attempt to exist on less than US$1.25 per day). They
include the diverse global multitudes who are deprived of their basic
human rights to enough food to survive and thrive, clean drinking
water, decent housing, education, and medical care. To our great
shame, this is the daily reality of over one billion of our brothers and
sisters in the world today.[8] For the purposes of this book, quantita-
tive statistics will be less useful than an appreciation of the personal

experience or *meaning* of poverty to the poor themselves. Leonardo and Clodovis Boff offer this qualitative definition of poverty from the perspective of the poor: "'Poor' for the people means dependence, debt, exposure, anonymity, contempt, and humiliation."[9]

Crucified peoples are oppressed by the systemic violence of life-threatening poverty and social exclusion, sometimes referred to as "structural violence" or "structural sin," but many members of these communities are also targeted for actual violent repression—especially if they somehow make it onto the list of those who are suspected of having an interest in changing unjust social conditions. "To the ugliness of daily poverty," says Sobrino, "is added the horror of torture."[10]

There are many historical and systemic forces that make certain communities poor and oppressed and *keep* them poor and oppressed. These dynamics, of course, usually center around efforts to keep money and power and privilege in the hands of a privileged minority, as opposed to a more just and equitable sharing of resources for all. This is the case not only within nations but also on the wider global scene. Ellacuría put it succinctly: "The oppression of the crucified people derives from a necessity in history: the necessity that many suffer so a few may enjoy, that many be dispossessed so a few may possess."[11]

THE SCOURGED CHRIST OF THE INDIES

Antonio de Montesinos was one of the first band of Spanish Dominican friars who came to the island of Hispaniola in 1510 to assist in the colonization and Christianization of its indigenous people. Hispaniola had been the home of the Taino people prior to the arrival of Christopher Columbus, who had "discovered" and claimed the "Indies" (Hispaniola and other Caribbean islands) for Spain a little less than twenty years before. The natives (whom Columbus called Indians) called their island home Ayiti—the origin of the name Haiti. Some five hundred years later, the former island home of the Taino is now shared by Haiti and the Dominican Republic—names that reveal both indigenous and conquistador origins.

Father Montesinos and his companions quickly found themselves appalled by the enslavement and abuse of the indigenous people by their colonial masters, especially by the oppressive *encomienda* system, which was designed to control and exploit native people for labor in mines and on the plantations of their bosses, the *encomenderos*. As many as three million Taino people lived on Hispaniola at the time the Spaniards arrived. Within thirty years, however, 85 percent of the population (about 2.5 million people) had died from violence, starvation, and diseases brought by the Spaniards (smallpox, typhus, influenza, measles) to which they had no resistance.[12]

At a mass on December 21, 1511, Montesinos preached a furious denunciation of the *encomienda* system. Notables from Hispaniola who were present that day included Admiral Diego Columbus (son of Christopher Columbus and governor of the island) and a number of other *encomenderos,* including a young man named Bartolomé de Las Casas (1484–1566), who later recorded Montesinos's scathing words:

> You are all in mortal sin! You live in it and die in it! Why? Because of the cruelty and tyranny you use with these innocent people. Tell me, with what right, with what justice, do you hold these Indians in such cruel and horrible servitude? On what authority have you waged such detestable wars on these people, in their mild, peaceful lands, where you have consumed such infinitudes of them, wreaking upon them this death and unheard-of havoc? How is it you hold them so crushed and exhausted, giving them nothing to eat, nor any treatment for their diseases, which you cause them to be infected with through the surfeit of their their toils, so that they may "die on you" [as you say]—you mean, you kill them—mining gold for you day after day? . . . Are these

not human beings? Have they no rational souls? Are you not
obligated to love them as you love yourselves? Do you not
understand this? Do you not grasp this? How is it that you
sleep so soundly, so lethargically?[13]

Although the words of Montesinos fell mostly on deaf ears, their
shocking truth had a profound, life-changing effect on Bartolomé
de Las Casas.[14] An *encomendero* himself, he gave up his property and
his indentured servants in 1514. Inspired by the example of Montesinos and others, he became a Dominican friar, and soon became
a fierce advocate for the human rights of the indigenous people of
Hispaniola and, eventually, of all the native peoples of the Americas
(New Spain), becoming known as the Protector of the Indians. Later
in life, when he was serving as bishop of Chiapas, Mexico, Las Casas
refused absolution to any Spaniard who refused to free his slaves.
Throughout his life he made trips back and forth to Spain to plead
with the Spanish authorities on behalf of the Indian peoples. With
the aim of exposing the rapacious cruelty of the Spanish conquest,
he wrote harrowing memoirs, including *A Brief Account of the Destruction of the Indies*, an eyewitness account that is not for the faint of
heart.[15] Five centuries later, the anguish, grief, and seething outrage
of Las Casas can be felt on every page.

Las Casas came to see the peoples of the Americas not as pagans
in need of conversion but as the embodiment of the tortured, crucified Christ, who was being disrespected and abused over and over
again in the indigenous peoples. It was the Spanish—who professed
Christianity but who obliviously went about their evil, un-Christian
business—whose souls were at stake and who needed conversion.
Las Casas wrote:

For I leave, in the Indies, Jesus Christ, our God, scourged and
afflicted and buffeted and crucified, not once but millions of
times, on the part of all the Spaniards who ruin and destroy
these people . . . depriving them of life before their time.[16]

The Taino people of Hispaniola were, for all intents and purposes, completely wiped out within the first century of the Spanish conquest. As they died out, however, the *encomenderos* had a continued need for slave labor, and so they began to import Africans to take the place of the diminishing Taino in the mines and in harvesting coffee, sugar, and other tropical produce. By 1540, some thirty thousand kidnapped Africans were already working as slaves on the island; they are the ancestors of the Afro-Caribbean people who now inhabit Haiti and the Dominican Republic.[17] The Africans were treated no better than the Taino. Accounts of their outrageous maltreatment and torture are horrifying, as evident in this account of an African slave by the name of Vastey:

> Have they not hung up men with heads downward, drowned them in sacks, crucified them on planks, buried them alive, crushed them in mortars? Have they not forced them to eat shit? And, after having flayed them with the lash, have they not cast them alive to be devoured by worms, or onto anthills, or lashed them to stakes in the swamp to be devoured by mosquitos? . . . Have they not consigned these miserable blacks to man-eating dogs, until the latter, sated by human flesh, left the mangled victims to be finished off by bayonet or poniard?[18]

Tragically, the story of the Indies was repeated all through Latin America. Eduardo Galeano has likened Europe—and, later, the United States—to a parasitic, vampire-like creature that has drained the lifeblood from Latin America for over five centuries. He means this both literally (millions of people actually deprived of life before their time by murder, poverty, being worked to death, and so on) and figuratively (innumerable boatloads of precious resources departing again and again, with little or no benefit to the masses of that exploited continent):

> Latin America is the region of open veins. Everything, from the discovery until our times, has always been transmuted

into European—or later United States—capital, and as such
has accumulated in distant centers of power. Everything: the
soil, its fruits and its mineral-rich depths, the people and their
capacity to work and to consume, natural resources and human resources. Production methods and class structure have
been successively determined from outside for each area by
meshing it into the universal gearbox of capitalism.[19]

A similar violent, predatory process occurred further north as
the continent of North America was conquered and confiscated by
the Europeans. Black Elk (1862–1950), a Lakota Sioux holy man,
spoke of the catastrophe that resulted from the encounter between
his people and the *Wasichus* (a Lakota word for white people of
European descent), especially after gold was discovered in the Black
Hills of South Dakota:

> The Wasichus had found much of the yellow metal that they
> worship and that makes them crazy, and they wanted to have
> a road up through our country to the place where the yellow
> metal was; but my people did not want the road. . . . Once we
> were happy in our own country and we were seldom hungry,
> for then the two-leggeds and the four-leggeds lived together
> like relatives, and there was plenty for them and for us. But the
> Wasichus came, and they made little islands for us and other
> little islands for the four-leggeds, and always these islands are
> becoming smaller, for around them surges the gnawing flood
> of the Wasichus; and it is dirty with lies and greed.[20]

KING LEOPOLD'S GHOST

Over the last few years I have come to know many lovely Congolese people through the Kovler Center. All speak both French
and at least one of the indigenous languages from this area of West

Central Africa. Because the Congolese community is not yet very well established in Chicago, a significant number of Congolese have ended up having to live in homeless shelters while they apply for political asylum in the United States. It goes without saying that the noise and insecurity and lack of privacy in such places are less than ideal for people who are suffering from post-traumatic stress.

There are actually *two* Congos, one on either side of the Congo River (the world's deepest river, and among the longest). The official name of the smaller Congo, to the west of the river, is the Republic of Congo, formerly known as the French Congo until its independence from France in 1960. The people commonly refer to their country as Congo-Brazzaville, after its capital city of Brazzaville.

The much larger Congo, to the east of the Congo River, is known as the Democratic Republic of Congo or simply DRC (except for the period from 1971 to 1997 when its name was changed to Zaire). It was known as the Belgian Congo until its independence from Belgium in 1960. The people from DRC commonly refer to it as Congo-Kinshasa, after its capital city of Kinshasa, which is immediately across the river from the neighboring capital of Brazzaville.

Prior to independence, Kinshasa was known as Leopoldville, a name with a dark story behind it. At a conference of European nations that was convened in Berlin in 1884 to sort out who would get to colonize which areas of Africa, King Leopold II of Belgium referred to the continent as a "magnificent cake" to be cut into portions for the Europeans. France was given a piece of the cake in the area west and north of the Congo River (now Congo-Brazzaville and the Central African Republic); Portugal was given a piece south of the river (now Angola). Bizarrely, King Leopold himself (*not* the country of Belgium) was given an enormous piece of the cake (905,000 square miles, now the DRC) east of the river, which he named the Congo Free State (1885–1908). This huge area (roughly one-fourth the size of the United States), became Leopold's privately owned and controlled colony for almost twenty-three years, until its administration was handed over to the country of Belgium, which renamed it the Belgian Congo (1908–60).

In *King Leopold's Ghost* Adam Hochschild recounts in excruciating detail how Leopold ran the Congo as his personal slave plantation. This was accomplished through the terrorizing violence of his private army, the Force Publique, which operated as an army of occupation and as a counterinsurgency force to put down rebellions, large and small, of people who refused to be exploited. But it mainly operated, according to Hochschild, as a "corporate labor police force" to bully and threaten and terrorize the indigenous population into performing slave labor to extract resources for export from the Congo.[21]

The officer corps of the Force Publique was composed entirely of white Europeans—a mix of soldiers drawn from the Belgian army along with paid mercenaries from other countries who were enticed by prospects of wealth and adventure in Africa. Regular soldiers were indigenous African conscripts or volunteers, who were ill paid and ill treated. Morale was low, desertions were common, and sometimes misery and resentment mounted to the point of mutinies against the European officers. African soldiers were stationed in areas at a distance from their home villages, according to the rationale that they might have fewer qualms about oppressing Africans from tribes other than their own. Typically, several dozen black soldiers were stationed under one or two white officers at garrisons at regular intervals along the Congo River or its tributaries.

Leopold amassed a huge personal fortune by extracting the rich natural resources of the Congo for his personal gain. These included ivory, copper, and other minerals, but most lucrative of all was the rubber trade—especially after the invention of the inflatable bicycle tire by J. B. Dunlop in 1887. Thousands upon thousands of rural villagers, as far as the Force Publique and the agents of the rubber traders could reach, were forced to become "rubber slaves." People were required, under threat of torture or death, to do the labor-intensive work of collecting sap from the rubber vines that grow wild on trees in the lush equatorial rain forest of the Congo. The task became even more labor intensive when vines close to the villages were "tapped out," which required rubber slaves to venture farther and farther into the forest to find new vines.

An 1892 entry from the journal of a Force Publique officer named Louis Chaltin is chilling: "The native does not like to make rubber. He must be compelled to do it."[22] Typical methods used to "compel" people to collect rubber were to pillage and loot their villages and kidnap the women—who would only be returned to their husbands and families after the requisite quota of rubber was delivered. If men refused, or if they did not meet the rubber quota, their wives and daughters were killed. The women were also subjected to other outrages while the distraught men were off in the rainforest collecting rubber sap: "The women taken during the last raid at Engwatta are causing me no end of trouble," wrote officer Georges Bricusse in his diary in 1895. "All the soldiers want one. The sentries who are supposed to guard them unchain the prettiest ones and rape them."[23]

If a village refused to submit to the demands of the rubber traders, people were shot to deliver an ultimatum to the villagers and anyone else in the surrounding area. A routine atrocity was to chop off the hands of uncooperative Africans—either while they were alive or after they were dead. Baskets of severed hands were carried back from expeditions to provide evidence to superiors that mercenaries and soldiers were doing their jobs. There was also a dreaded instrument of punishment that came to be synonymous with white rule: the *chicotte*, a whip made of dried hippopotamus hide. Each lash left permanent scars on the buttocks or back or legs. Twenty-five lashes caused unconsciousness; a hundred lashes (not uncommon) could be fatal. Stanislas LeFranc, a magistrate in Leopoldville, was repulsed by the chicotte:

> The station chief selects the victims. . . . Trembling, haggard,
> they lie face down on the ground. . . . Each time the torturer

lifts up the *chicotte,* a reddish stripe appears on the skin of the pitiful victims, who, however firmly held, gasp in frightful contortions. . . . At the first blows the unhappy victims let out horrible cries which soon become faint groans. . . . In a refinement of evil, some officers, and I've witnessed this, demand that when the sufferer gets up, panting, he must graciously give the military salute.[24]

The population of the Congo Free State was estimated at twenty million at the time Leopold and his minions took over. During the Leopold period and in its immediate aftermath, however, the population dropped by *half*—by approximately *ten million people.* Hochschild devotes an entire chapter to the evidence for this unimaginable holocaust of millions of human souls.[25] He identifies four primary causes:

1. *Murder.*
2. *Starvation, exhaustion, and exposure.* These factors were especially lethal for displaced people who fled raided villages and died in the forest, and for people who were worked to death.
3. *Disease.* Similar to what happened to the indigenous peoples of the Americas, Europeans brought diseases to the Congo, including smallpox, to which the people had no resistance.
4. *Plummeting birth rate.* "Not surprisingly," writes Hochschild, "when men were sent into the forest in search of rubber for weeks at a time, year after year, and women were held hostage and half-starved, fewer children were born." It was also harder for women to run and hide from slave drivers if they were pregnant or had to carry young children along.[26]

Eventually, thanks to a number of concerned missionaries and journalists, reports of the atrocities in the Congo began to make the newspapers in Europe and America, and an international movement for human rights in the Congo began to take shape. E. D. Morel, a young clerk for a British shipping company, observed on a trip to Belgium that ships arriving from Congo were laden with valuable cargo, such as ivory and rubber, but for their return journey they were loaded with guns, chains, ammunition, and explosives. In the late 1800s and early 1900s Morel wrote a series of articles to expose the enslavement and abuse of people in the Congo. Roger Casement, British consul for the Congo, conducted an investigation and wrote a scathing report in 1904. Casement encouraged Morel to found the Congo Reform Association, which had the support of famous writers like Mark Twain, who published a biting, satirical pamphlet titled *King Leopold's Soliloquy* in 1905. The international outcry eventually led to the administration of the Congo being transferred from King Leopold to the country of Belgium in 1908, when it was renamed the Belgian Congo.

Another writer who lent his support to the movement for human rights in the Congo was Joseph Conrad, whose 1899 novel, *The Heart of Darkness,* is actually based on a personal journey he took up the Congo River in the early 1890s. "And this," says Marlow, a character in the novel who prepares the travelers (and readers) for the horrors they will encounter on their steamboat ride up the river, "has been one of the dark places of the earth." Marlow reflects on the motivations of the "conquerors" of the Congo:

> They were conquerors, and for that you want only brute force—nothing to boast of, when you have it, since your strength is just an accident arising from the weakness of others. They grabbed what they could get for the sake of what was to be got. It was just robbery with violence, aggravated murder on a great scale, and men going at it blind—as is very proper for those who tackle a darkness. The conquest of the earth, which mostly means the taking it away from those who have a different complexion or slightly flatter noses than ourselves, is not a pretty thing when you look into it too much. What

redeems it is the idea only. An idea at the back of it; not a sentimental pretense but an idea; and an unselfish belief in the idea—something you can set up, and bow down before, and offer a sacrifice to.[27]

The "idea," which seems to operate as a kind of idolatrous false god "at the back" of the whole thing, centers around *money*: worship of it, obsession with it, bowing down before it, putting ourselves at the service of it—even to the point of rationalizing the sacrifice of human lives in order to get more and more *of* it. "Like all false gods," writes Elizabeth Johnson, "money and its trappings require the sacrifice of victims. Whether the poor are offered up indirectly through the economic conditions necessary to produce profit, or directly through the violence necessary to sustain these conditions, their lives are the sacrifice."[28]

The great sacrifice of lives in the Congo was not, strictly speaking, a genocide. Leopold and his minions were not out to kill people; they simply didn't care whether they lived or died. Their goal was to make the maximum profit possible, as quickly as possible, by exploiting vulnerable people for slave labor. Deaths were incidental—as long as there were other live bodies to replace them so the work could get done. African lives did not count.

King Leopold's ghost continues to haunt the people of the Democratic Republic of Congo; reverberations of this massive historical trauma are felt on every level of their personal and social existence today. Since 1996, as many as five million people have died in a complex and brutal civil war that has been called "the world's worst war."[29] The war is particularly notorious for the widespread, systematic practice of mass rape by marauding militias. Sadly, the rich natural resources of the DRC (diamonds, copper, uranium, cobalt, gold, zinc, tungsten, coltan, tin) play a role in fueling the violence; armed groups finance themselves through illicit trade of valuable minerals from the mines. Congolese uranium is a source of particular interest and concern (radioactive material for the atomic bombs dropped on Hiroshima and Nagasaki was mined in Congo), with the risk that black-market uranium will get into the hands of bad actors.

Rich deposits of minerals that are used to make electronic components of cell phones and laptop computers (coltan, tin, tungsten) also make the DRC very attractive to a lucrative industry that is driven by insatiable consumer demand for ever more "smart" and interesting gadgets. Sadly, it is easy for us to remain oblivious to the connection between the pleasure our electronic devices give us and the misery of the Congo—even if it as close to us as the cell phone at our ear.[30]

DISORDERED PRIORITIES AND STUPID DEATHS

Paul Farmer, a US physician who has devoted his life to caring for the poorest of the poor, often expresses dismay in his talks and writings that millions of men, women, and children around the world have to die needlessly every year from treatable illnesses—in most cases simply *because* they are poor:

> Ten million people—many of them young and most of them poor—will die around the world this year from diseases for which safe, affordable, effective treatments exist. In Haiti these are known as "stupid deaths." What's more, inadequate medical care predominates precisely where the burden of disease is heaviest, keeping a billion souls from leading full lives in good health.[31]

The first priority of Farmer and Partners In Health (PIH), the organization he co-founded in 1987, is to prevent such "stupid deaths" by finding creative ways to get health care to people who need it the most. "These deaths," says Farmer, "are a great injustice and a stain on the conscience of modern medicine and science."[32] Drawing inspiration from liberation theology, the aim of PIH is to provide a "preferential option for the poor" in health care. "By establishing long-term relationships with sister organizations based in settings of poverty," reads its mission statement, "Partners In Health strives to achieve two overarching goals: to bring the benefits of modern science to those most in need of them and to serve as an antidote to despair. . . . At its root, our mission is both medical and moral. It is based on solidarity, rather than charity alone."

PIH began by providing creative, community-based medical treatment in Haiti's Central Plateau region, which included training members of the local community to implement care and treatment for patients too ill to travel or in need of personal, home-based care. By the early 1990s the Haiti program was caring for 100,000 patients a year. One remarkable innovation was facilitated by Farmer's colleague Dr. Jim Kim, who was instrumental in cutting deals on otherwise prohibitively expensive drugs, making it possible to get them to poor people suffering from tuberculosis, HIV/AIDS, and other infectious diseases. The PIH program has since grown considerably and is now providing health care in Haiti, Peru, Rwanda, Lesotho, Malawi, Mexico, Guatemala, Russia, the Dominican Republic, Kazakhstan, and the United States (inner-city Boston and the Navaho Nation).

Paul Farmer is primarily concerned with saving lives. He is also concerned, though, with understanding why, as ten million people continue to die needless, preventable deaths every year, "the world goes on as if nothing much has happened." And so it is important "to look for a better comprehension of the social causes of horror and also of our tolerance of societal abominations."[33] Becoming too comfortable with the inequitable distribution of resources in our world—too tolerant of "societal abominations"—is a particular moral and spiritual hazard for people from situations of relative privilege,. "The quickest way to lose your humanity," says William Sloane Coffin," is to begin to tolerate the intolerable."[34] One indication that we are losing our humanity is obliviousness to suffering occurring in the rest of the world:

The voices, the faces, the suffering of the sick and the poor are all around us. Can we see and hear them? Well-defended against troubling incursions of doubt, we the privileged are precisely the people most at risk of remaining oblivious, since this kind of suffering is not central to our own experience.[35]

There are ways that the comfort and convenience afforded by our privilege can have a direct relationship with the suffering of others—even when they are at a great distance from us, and even while we remain oblivious to it. Stupid deaths happen all the time. As I write, bodies of garment workers are still being recovered from the rubble of the Rana Plaza building that collapsed on April 24, 2013, in Dhaka, Bangladesh. So far, over 1,127 dead have been confirmed, many young women in their late teens or early twenties who were stitching clothes in the five garment factories housed in the building, which was known to be a death trap prior to its collapse.[36] The factories were part of a booming garment industry in Bangladesh that has become very competitive in the global export market (second only to China) by offering some of the cheapest labor on the planet. At the time of the disaster, the legal minimum wage for garment workers was three thousand taka (about US$38 dollars a month). Bangladesh now has about five thousand such factories employing approximately four million workers. Contracts are worked out with huge companies (Walmart, Target, and others) that are able to take advantage of sinfully cheap labor in developing countries to produce clothing that can be sold in large quantities at low prices for large profits. A few days after the Rana disaster, with images of distraught and grieving people at the site of the collapsed building still in the headlines, I was shopping for a shirt and found one that I liked at a very good price. A little voice whispered to me that I ought to check the tag for where it came from; it read "Made in Bangladesh." I winced, thinking for a moment of the Bangladeshi workers, but then quickly put them out of my mind and bought the shirt. Paul Farmer summarizes the process this way: "The cognitive dissonance between, on the one hand, the overwhelming suffering of the poor and, on the other, our attachment to our own way of life, makes turning away and 'not seeing' quite understandable human behavior. It stands to reason that, as beneficiaries of growing inequality, we don't like to be reminded of misery and squalor and failure."[37]

Disordered priorities in how nations spend their money are also a major cause of stupid deaths. Positive correlations between numbers of dead human beings and expenditures for weapons and war making are obvious. For example, the National Priorities Project, which carefully tracks both military and non-military budget outlays in the United States, has calculated that, as of summer 2013, the United States has officially appropriated nearly *one trillion dollars* to fund the up-front costs of the Iraq war.[38] Although US troops were officially withdrawn from Iraq in 2011, the long-term costs of the war will eventually end up being at least *three trillion dollars* (and probably much more). These include astronomical interest payments, for years to come, on the trillion dollars that was borrowed to fund a war that we were unable to pay for. There are also the hundreds of billions of dollars, for years to come, to pay the medical bills and disability benefits for over fifty-eight thousand US soldiers who were wounded, and for easily one hundred thousand more who are suffering from invisible wounds like post-traumatic stress disorder, major depression, and traumatic brain injury.[39] In addition, the Department of Defense has confirmed that 4,477 US soldiers have died since the start of the Iraq war.

Civilian deaths are harder to estimate. Shortly after the March 2003 invasion, when asked about civilian casualties, US General Tommy Franks responded, "We don't do body counts." Iraq Body Count, a group that *has* felt the need to keep track of the mounting death toll, has conservatively estimated (and likely underestimated) Iraqi civilian casualties resulting from the US invasion and occupation (including the bloody sectarian mayhem it set in motion) as between 112,000 and 123,000 dead.[40] Other estimates are much higher. One study, published in the *Lancet* medical journal by researchers from Johns Hopkins University and Al Mustansiriya University in Baghdad, estimated over 600,000 "excess" Iraqi civilian deaths over the first three years of the war: "We estimate that between March 18, 2003, and June 2006, an additional 654,965 Iraqis have died above what would have been expected on the basis of the pre-invasion crude mortality rate as a consequence of the coalition invasion. Of these deaths, we estimate that 601,027 were due to violence."[41] There have been critiques of the methodology of this study and concerns that it may have overestimated civilian casualties. But since the Iraq war itself was unnecessary, illegal, and unjust, the inarguable bottom line is that *each* and *every* Iraqi death—whether a hundred thousand or six-hundred thousand or a million—was unnecessary, a death that did not have to happen, a stupid death.

There are also all the needless deaths that are caused *indirectly* by weapons and war making, because precious funds and resources that could be used for constructive, life-enhancing, life-saving purposes are diverted into preparing for war or making war. The breakdown of the projected US Federal Budget for the year 2014 gives a clear picture of our disordered national priorities. According to the National Priorities Project website, of the 1.15 trillion dollars available for "discretionary spending" (that is, not already committed for mandatory spending on things like Social Security, Medicare, veterans' benefits, interest on national debt, and so on), *630 billion dollars* (56.5 percent) will be spent on the military. By comparison, 60 billion (5.2 percent) will be spent on health and 74 billion (6.4 percent) on education.

In his prophetic "Beyond Vietnam" speech at the Riverside Church in New York City on April 4, 1967, Dr. Martin Luther King Jr. spoke of his grief and disappointment that a needless, unjust war in Southeast Asia was undermining and draining precious resources away from efforts to fight poverty and injustice at home in the United States:

There is at the outset a very obvious and almost facile connection between the war in Vietnam and the struggle I, and
others, have been waging in America. A few years ago there
was a shining moment in that struggle. It seemed as if there
was a real promise of hope for the poor—both black and
white—through the poverty program. Then came the buildup
in Vietnam, and I watched this program broken and eviscerat-
ed, as if it were some idle political plaything of a society gone
mad on war, and I knew that America would never invest the
necessary funds or energies in rehabilitation of its poor so long
as adventures like Vietnam continued to draw men and skills
and money like some demonic destructive suction tube. So, I
was increasingly compelled to see the war as an enemy of the
poor and to attack it as such.

One year later, to the day, Dr. King was assassinated in Memphis,
Tennessee.

This chapter concludes with a couple of poems that seem fitting.
The first, "From the Bridge," by Nicaraguan poet Claribel Alegria,
is very sad:

> I never found the order
> I searched for
> but always a sinister
> and well-planned disorder
> that increases in the hands
> of those who hold power
> while the others
> who clamor for
> a more kindly world,
> a world with less hunger
> and more hopefulness,
> die of torture
> in the prisons.[42]

The second, holding more hope in things unseen, is an excerpt from James Russell Lowell's poem "The Present Crisis," written in 1844, which was one of Dr. King's favorites:

> Truth forever on the scaffold,
> Wrong forever on the throne
> Yet that scaffold sways the future,
> And, behind the dim unknown
> Standeth God within the shadow
> Keeping watch above his own.[43]

4

THE WOUNDS OF TORTURE
Whoever Was Tortured, Stays Tortured

In the long months of confinement, I often thought of how to transmit the pain that a tortured person undergoes. And always I concluded it was impossible.
—Jacobo Timmerman[1]

JEAN AMERY, A participant in the Belgian resistance movement against the Nazis during the Second World War, was captured and brutally tortured by the Gestapo before being sent to a concentration camp. After narrowly surviving the horrors of the camps, he went on to live another thirty years. Eventually though, and slowly, he succumbed to despair, finally dying by suicide in 1978. In his remarkable book *At the Mind's Limits: Contemplations of a Survivor of Auschwitz and Its Realities,* he describes the harrowing experience of torture and the ways it haunted him for the rest of his life. Although he recovered in time from his bodily injuries, the wounds to his psyche and spirit never really seemed to heal. "Whoever was tortured," he wrote, "stays tortured."[2]

In this chapter I explore the wounds of torture to bodies, minds, hearts, souls, families, and communities. Some wounds are visible, obviously evident in the scars, limps, and disfigurements that some survivors carry with them for the rest of their lives. Other wounds are invisible, yet nonetheless real and distressing. Repercussions can undermine the morale of whole communities and can even be passed on to future generations. Potentials for healing and redemption after torture are explored in later chapters; this one dwells on the damage it does.

TWENTY-FIRST CENTURY STIGMATA

One young survivor living in exile in the United States was quite fragile; he was unable to hold a job and had been in and out of psychiatric hospitals multiple times. In his homeland he had been an aspiring musician and songwriter. Once, when feeling upset about rampant political corruption and repression in his country, he wrote a protest song to express his feelings. This was considered subversive by the authorities, and he was soon taken in for questioning. The interrogators repeatedly taunted him about the insolence he had displayed by saying (singing) things that were critical of the government. "*So you want to be a prophet? You want to be like Jesus Christ?*" And, as the young man was restrained by guards, the interrogator brandished a hammer and proceeded to pound a chisel into his hand and his foot. A doctor's forensic report, submitted in support of his application for political asylum to document medical evidence of torture, verified the stigmata. Like Jesus, he would ever after be known "by the marks where the nails have been."[3]

Many people are physically injured by their torturers, which can result in scars or disfigurements or painful physical conditions that they carry with them for the rest of their lives. Doctors who assess medical evidence of torture must precisely measure scars on various parts of the body in order to document whether a survivor's injuries are consistent with the stories they tell about what happened to them. The catalogue of possible injuries is limited only by the bounds of the perverse imaginations and grotesque improvisations of the torturers. Torture violates the basic bodily integrity of the person. "The body," writes Judith Herman, "is invaded, injured, defiled."[4] It seems in poor taste to give too many examples; a few will suffice to give a feeling for how the body remembers what it went through.

Perhaps the most common form of torture is *beating*. Some are beaten to death. People are hit in the head with batons or rifle butts, kicked in the head or body, punched in the face. They end up with bruises, lacerations, broken bones, broken teeth, back injuries, head injuries, internal injuries. Sometimes a person's head is deliberately pounded against the wall or the floor; sometimes people inadvertently strike their head when they fall down or when they are knocked down. Some lose consciousness for moments, minutes, or days; some suffer concussions or traumatic brain injury. I recently met a woman whose head was violently slammed into a table by an interrogator; years later, her face registered a look of profound disappointment and disbelief that someone could actually do such a thing. I know several people whose family members died of brain injuries sustained during torture. One young man lost his father, who was viciously beaten by police during a nonviolent political demonstration; he went into a coma from which he never emerged.

Persistent headaches are a common symptom of both head trauma and psychological trauma. During an initial interview with a man who had been clubbed on the head by police, I remember how he began to grimace and clutch his head as he recalled emotionally charged memories. At a certain point we had to stop the interview because his head hurt so much that he thought he was going to be sick. He had suffered like this for years. Thankfully, within just a few days he was able to experience tremendous relief from medications that can be remarkably effective in treating such pain and anxiety. A few weeks later he was able to tell his story without this kind of disabling distress.

Some prisoners become gravely ill or develop serious medical problems because of the inhumane conditions under which they are held; in some cases these conditions are tantamount to torture.

Prisoners may be deprived of adequate food or water, or they may be provided with dirty water or spoiled food that makes them sick. They may not be allowed to bathe and may become infested with vermin. Some become terribly sick from infections that develop in unsanitary conditions. They may be kept in places with no bathroom facilities except for a disgusting bucket that is shared with no privacy by many people in an overcrowded cell. One young soldier, whose only offense was questioning unjust orders, was held for nearly two years in a military prison with no opportunity to brush his teeth. When his teeth started to decay, he developed unbearable toothaches. His cell mates had to help him figure out how to pull some of his own teeth.

Prisoners can also be deprived of needed medical care—either for injuries from their torture or for sicknesses they develop while they are detained. One man, whose testicle was crushed and whose ureter was damaged by vicious kicks to his genital area, was left languishing in agony on the floor of his cell for ten days before he was allowed to get medical attention. His injuries were so severe that immediate surgical intervention was required; it should have occurred ten days earlier. He was on a catheter for over a month.

Sexual trauma is also very common among torture survivors. Some torturers are inclined to sexually punish and humiliate their captives. We see this kind of thing in the obscene photographs of naked prisoners from Abu Ghraib. Rape, including gang rape, is an especially common form of violent indignity to which female prisoners are subjected. On top of this, some rape victims end up with sexually transmitted diseases. They may also become pregnant by their rapists. Rape happens to men, too. In my clinical work with a number of male torture survivors, one of the presenting problems has been chronic rectal pain and bleeding that resulted from anal rape—sometimes with objects like pipes or the muzzle of a rifle.

Psychological trauma is sometimes experienced in the form of painful physical symptoms. Survivors may suffer tension headaches, gastrointestinal problems, or cardiac problems that are triggered or aggravated by anxiety and stress. Many lose their appetite. Perhaps the most prevalent symptom is chronic, severe insomnia. Most torture survivors have trouble falling asleep or staying asleep. Their sleep is often disturbed by terrifying nightmares, which can be so vivid that they resemble flashbacks, in which the experience of torture is relived. I remember once trying to conduct an interview with a man who was so totally exhausted from lack of sleep that he would nod off repeatedly in mid-sentence. It turned out that he had had almost no sleep for weeks. For him, surrendering to sleep felt dangerous, because he was inevitably awakened by nightmares in which he was surrounded by his torturers. Another man, who often awoke screaming and flailing, kept a bible by his bedside; the only thing that helped him recover some sense of composure was to touch the sacred book in the middle of the night. Eventually, with the help of medication, both of these men began to sleep more peacefully, for which they were profoundly grateful.

BROKEN HEARTS, BROKEN SPIRITS

Whether or not torture results in serious bodily injury, it always causes invisible wounds to the mind and spirit. Such injuries can be very deep, making it hard to tell where emotional pain leaves off and spiritual pain begins. Torture is a heartbreaking experience, but on a deeper level it can break the spirit, potentially leading to a loss of faith in God, humanity, and the world.

The humiliation and indignity of torture can profoundly un-dermine the self-esteem of the survivor. People who are treated poorly usually end up feeling poorly about themselves; those who are disrespected are at risk of losing self-respect. They are also at risk for developing deeper problems on the level of the soul. "One of the most blasphemous consequences of injustice and prejudice," says Desmond Tutu, "is that it can make a child of God doubt that he or she is a child of God."[5] In *Horrendous Evils and the Goodness of God* Marilyn McCord Adams describes the sense of damage and

defilement at the core of a person's being that can result from being subjected to extreme cruelty. The destructive power of such
experiences, she says, reaches "into the deep structure of the person's frameworks for meaning-making, seemingly to defeat the
individual's value as a person, to degrade him/her to subhuman
status."[6] One feels less than human, less worthy of the respect that
is owed to a child of God.

Torture undermines the foundations of security and trust that
the world can be counted on to be a reasonably safe and decent
place. "The sense of safety in the world, or basic trust, is acquired in
earliest life," writes Judith Herman. "It forms the basis of all systems
of relationship and faith. The original experience of care makes it
possible for human beings to envisage a world in which they be-
long, a world hospitable to human life."[7] Torture, the antithesis of
care and hospitality, shatters this sense of basic trust. "Whoever has
succumbed to torture," writes Amery, "can no longer feel at home
in the world."[8]

The emotional pain of torture survivors originates in the terror
and powerlessness they experienced when they were at the mercy
of their torturers. "Psychological trauma is an affliction of the pow-
erless," says Herman. "At the moment of trauma, the victim is ren-
dered helpless by overwhelming force." There is no way to escape,
no way to defend oneself or fight back. "Traumatic reactions occur
when action is of no avail. When neither resistance nor escape is
possible, the human system of self-defense becomes overwhelmed
and disorganized."[9] Anxiety and horror take over.

Every torture survivor is a unique individual with particular
strengths and vulnerabilities, and so survivors do not always fit neatly
into diagnostic categories like PTSD.[10] Most, however, do report
painful inner experiences that resemble at least some of the classic
symptoms of PTSD. These fall into three general categories: (1) persistent anxiety and expectation of danger *(hyperarousal)*; (2) disturbing
memories and reexperiencing of traumatic events *(intrusion)*; and (3)

emotional numbing, a diminished capacity to feel as a way to cope with unbearable feelings *(constriction)*.

Hyperarousal is a heightened state of anxiety and vigilance for danger and harm that can persist long after a traumatic experience like torture. It is as if the body's system of self-preservation (tensing in response to danger, preparing to fight or run) becomes locked into a state of perpetual alert. Some survivors are ever on the lookout for bad actors with malicious intentions; they may be fearful of being followed or under surveillance. Some seem to become frozen in the "fight or flight" response that was originally experienced during the horrors of torture, but which is now an ongoing state of chronic, debilitating tension. It is simply not possible to relax. The result is emotional and physical exhaustion.

Intrusive, disturbing memories of past traumatic experiences are also very common. Emotionally charged images of torture continue to come, unbidden, into the survivor's consciousness, disrupting concentration or sleep. These could be auditory memories of people screaming under torture, or visual images of the contemptuous face of a torturer. The traumatic past intrudes upon the present, undermining the survivor's efforts to function and move on. Even sleep may not be a refuge because, instead of restorative rest, survivors are tormented by nightmares of being back in the dungeon they thought they had escaped.

Flashbacks are the most extreme form of intrusive memory. Past experiences are not only recalled but are *relived* in the present. Sometimes certain situations or stimuli can evoke or trigger traumatic memories. A police or military uniform, a sight or sound or smell associated with torture, can bring it all back. Sister Dianna Ortiz, whose torture included being repeatedly burned with cigarettes, could not smell cigarette smoke without being reminded of her torture. A woman who was raped by soldiers smelling of alcohol could not be around people who were drinking without images of rape coming into her mind. The joy of sexual intimacy may be spoiled by memories of sexual trauma. One Guatemalan woman offered this testimony:

> "Now I am old, because of the war and having suffered so much. I can no longer work because I am so ill. The rape really left me affected. I have never again been able to be with a man. The humiliation was so great. So, I tried to forget. I never talked about this before. Because of the shame, I don't want people to know."[11]

Another common feature of post-traumatic stress is emotional constriction or numbing, which has to do with the survivor's efforts to keep uncomfortable and disturbing feelings out of consciousness. Robert Jay Lifton refers to this as *psychic numbing.* "At the heart of the traumatic syndrome—and of the overall human struggle with pain—is the diminished capacity to feel, or psychic numbing."[12] This is a way for the survivor to cope with unbearable feelings about unbearable experiences. Some may alternate between emotional disconnection from themselves and being overwhelmed from within by terrible feelings and memories.

Profound grief is another central feature in the emotional landscape of survivors. The grief arises not as a direct result of torture but from the multiple losses that ensue from it—beginning with a painful break from life as they knew it before torture. Things will never be the same; *they* will never be the same. If survivors are able to come home, they may seem very different. *He is not himself. She is not herself.* Some are never able to return home. They must go into hiding for months or years. And many must make the heartbreaking decision to flee their homelands and go into exile.

WOUNDED FAMILIES AND COMMUNITIES

Families and communities suffer in many different ways when their loved ones are persecuted and tortured. They are wounded through their relationship and connection with the tortured person.

This begins with a sense of unbearable anguish and suspense when a family member or friend disappears or is taken away by the authorities. This is especially the case when it is widely known that some people never come back or that those who do come back may never be the same because they have been so badly treated. Families and friends pray and hope for the best but must prepare for the worst. Things can end very badly.

Sometimes family members end up getting themselves into trouble by pleading with authorities about their loved ones who have been detained. They may themselves be threatened or tortured as a means of coercing the detained person to confess or give up information. Some are injured or killed during violent scenes when soldiers or police are taking a loved one away. One man recalled how his father tried to intervene as he was being dragged out of the house; the older gentleman was shot and killed in front of the whole family. Some months later, after the same man managed to escape and went into hiding, soldiers paid a visit to his home and raped his wife.

Another man, a thoughtful, soft-spoken medical researcher, had been pressured by authorities to falsify results of a scientific study that would embarrass the government. At great cost to himself and his family, he refused to violate his professional ethics. On the night he was taken from his home, he was made to witness the rape of his pregnant wife by a group of soldiers. Even more awful, his little daughter was also present. The little girl began to protest loudly to try to get the men to stop doing bad things to her mommy. In annoyance, a soldier viciously kicked her in the head. The little girl died from her head injury at the scene; the mother and her unborn child died a few hours later. When asked some typical clinical questions to assess intrusive thoughts and memories of these traumatic events, the man responded that he has been haunted most by the unforgettable sound of his daughter screaming, "Daddy! Daddy!" He wept quietly.

Families often suffer great financial hardship as a result of the torture of their loved ones. Sometimes the detained person is the breadwinner, which leaves the family in precarious or desperate circumstances. Long imprisonments of a spouse or parent can result in traumatized families being overwhelmed with financial stress and overloaded by responsibilities. Some torture survivors may no longer have a job when they return home, or they may not be in emotional or physical shape to return to work. Sometimes survivors who were professionals in their homelands must go into exile, perhaps ending up washing dishes or working minimum wage jobs in the United States. Nonetheless, they wire staggering percentages of their modest wages back home to support their families.

Family members of the disappeared have unique and complex problems with grief. Ongoing uncertainty about the whereabouts and well-being of their loved ones makes it difficult or impossible to resolve their grief and thereby experience at least some measure of emotional closure. After months or years, even if it is almost certain that the *desaparecido* is dead, they may yet cling to hopes that he or she is still alive. Even if they eventually resign themselves to the likelihood of death, they never get the chance to see the body, to go through normal mourning rituals, or to have the consolation of giving them a decent burial and knowing where they rest. This has been a huge problem in Guatemala, where over fifty thousand people are known to have been disappeared by the government and its agents. For years, numerous organizations have been carefully and respectfully exhuming the remains of the murdered and disappeared from hundreds of mass graves and clandestine cemeteries all around the country. The purpose of the exhumations is twofold. First, the remains are examined to obtain forensic evidence of how the person died (for example, bullet holes or evidence of trauma to bones or skulls); these are, after all, *crime* scenes. Second, efforts are made to identify the remains, whenever possible, so they can be returned to their families and communities for decent burial.

Sometimes families and communities turn to unhealthy means of coping with loss and trauma. "To deal with our ghosts, our monsters, the pain, the suffering," said one person interviewed by the Guatemalan Commission for Historical Clarification, "people now kill themselves with drinking, because no one has been able to process their experiences. Those that do not have the capacity to cry, hold their tears and cry inside."[13] Whole communities may develop a host of problems in response to massive group trauma and unresolved historical grief, undermining their morale and impeding the process of collective healing and recovery.[14]

In some situations the actual motives for torture go well beyond obtaining information or confession from individuals. The broader strategy is to intimidate opposition and resistance, to terrorize whole communities into submission. "Torture as an instrument of political and social control," writes Bill Gorman, "is intended to rob its victims of their 'voice' and their agency, to have them serve as abject warnings to the general populace."[15] Torture silences and disables individual victims, but it can also be quite effective in silencing and disabling the communities from which they come. About the situation in Chile under the brutal Pinochet regime, Bill Cavanaugh writes: "The intended target of torture was not so much individual bodies but social bodies that would rival the state's power. Torture spread fear in the body politic, and people learned to keep to themselves and avoid contact with others."[16] Such inhibition and withdrawal can have tragic consequences: human potential is wasted, young leaders don't come forward, just causes are not advanced, important work does not get done, prophetic words remain unspoken, and good people are tempted to give up trying.

5

CARING FOR TORTURE SURVIVORS

I'm Still Here

I'm still here. A minute of silence for me.
—Izet Sarajlic[1]

DR. MARY FABRI, a clinical psychologist with a deep sense of social conscience, was one of several medical and mental-health professionals who were struck by the large numbers of severely traumatized people from Latin America, especially from El Salvador and Guatemala, who were seeking care at Chicago's Cook County Hospital in the middle 1980s. Many were reluctant to talk about what had happened to them in their homeland. One of Fabri's physician colleagues, Dr. Irene Martinez, who herself was a survivor of torture from Argentina's "Dirty War," suspected that some of these patients were survivors of torture. "I thought they were torture survivors," she explained, "because they reminded me of *me*."[2] Eventually, a small treatment program was launched to care for the unique and complex needs of these patients; it would later become the Heartland Alliance Marjorie Kovler Center for the Treatment of Survivors of Torture, which has become a unique place of healing and sanctuary for torture survivors in the Chicago area. Dr. Fabri,

an unusually creative and compassionate psychotherapist, helped
to mentor and nurture the Kovler Center program for twenty-five
years, until her retirement in 2012.

In this chapter I explore some of the unique challenges of caring
for torture survivors. This always begins with efforts to provide, as
much as possible, some measure of safety and support. These can
encompass anything from helping a survivor find a secure place to
live to creating the kind of emotional climate that makes it possible for any kind of healing to occur. The process of recovery is
fraught with anxiety and grief, sometimes requiring that survivors
remember and talk about things they wish they could just forget.
I also offer some thoughts on the ups and downs of those who
care for torture survivors; these include the emotional hazards of
vicarious traumatization, but also the feelings of joy and inspiration
experienced by those who have the privilege of accompanying these
courageous, resilient people on their journey of recovery.

SANCTUARY AND HOSPITALITY

Establishing a sense of safety is the first priority in work with torture survivors, whose experiences have left them feeling profoundly
unsafe and insecure.[3] First of all, they need *sanctuary*. The original
Latin meanings of the word suggest both "a place of refuge or
protection" and "a holy place." In the Middle Ages fugitives were
immune from arrest when they sought sanctuary in churches and
other sacred places.

In their home country, when survivors have managed to get out
of prison, their immediate problem is to find refuge and protection
from further harm and persecution. If they remain under threat
of being rearrested, and it is not safe to return home, a safe hiding
place must be found where they can recuperate from their injuries
and try to recover some sense of emotional composure. Basic needs
for food, stable housing, and medical care must be met. Privacy is
very important to people whose bodily integrity has been violated;

peace and quiet are also essential for people whose nerves are shot, and who are usually unable to sleep well.

Sometimes the crisis of detention mobilizes families and communities to go to extraordinary and even heroic lengths to release and rescue people who have been detained. People get organized, send out the word. Visits are made to authorities. Money is raised to pay bribes to people who might be in a position to arrange for release, or who could be persuaded to leave a door unlocked or look the other way while the prisoner makes a run for it. When it is too dangerous for survivors to return to their own homes, generous people often allow their homes or churches or mosques to be used as hiding places until the danger passes or until arrangements can be made for the survivors to be smuggled out of the country.

It is awe inspiring to witness how many angels of mercy, unsung heroes, and saints seem to rise to the occasion and come forward in these dangerous and desperate situations. So many stories come to mind: A doctor who smuggled a severely injured man out of a hospital in the middle of the night so he could avoid being returned to prison for further torture—with a priest waiting outside to drive him to safety. People arranging meetings at clandestine places to help endangered persons evade capture and move them further along the underground railroad. All kinds of clever lies and stories cooked up to get endangered people through military roadblocks. A soldier with an uneasy conscience, ordered to execute a prisoner in the woods, who instead shot his rifle into the air and encouraged the man to run for his life. In the Christian tradition those who allow torture survivors to stay for days or months or years in churches, parsonages, rectories, convents, and homes embody a long and deep tradition of providing hospitality and sanctuary. "Do not neglect to show hospitality to strangers, for by doing that some have entertained angels without knowing it. Remember those who are in prison, as though you were in prison with them; those who are being tortured, as though you yourselves were being tortured" (Heb 13:2–3).

When there are indications that the authorities are continuing to search for survivors (for example, agents showing up at their home or work place), or if they simply can't take it any longer, the only safe choice may be for them to leave the country. In many cases this is not possible because sufficient financial resources or social support are not available or because the security situation is so tightly controlled. In such situations survivors must stay and do the best they can, for better or for worse, in a scary climate of ongoing threat and danger. Others find ways to flee their homeland and go into exile, sometimes having to leave family and loved ones under emergency circumstances without any kind of emotional preparation to say goodbye. Jobs, homes, careers, culture, communities—everyone and everything that was secure and familiar—must be left behind. Heartbroken mothers must leave their children; fathers who prided themselves on providing for their families suffer deep anguish when they are unable to do so. A sad line from an old Irish ballad comes to mind:

> Regardless of the children's cries,
> the mothers' tears, the fathers' sighs;
> in thousands we are driven from home,
> which grieves our hearts full sore.[4]

For some who are driven from home, leaving their country may mean crossing the border to a refugee camp or a city in a neighboring country. Such border crossings can be quite risky, requiring evasion of border police or hikes across rugged and dangerous terrain. Some embark on even more ambitious and harrowing journeys to faraway lands. For example, we have seen a remarkable number of young men from East African countries like Eritrea, Somalia, and Ethiopia who have found their way by plane from Africa to South America, and who then make their way by land through Central America and Mexico all the way to the US border. There, they turn themselves in to US border patrol agents and request political asylum in the United States. They usually spend months in immigration detention centers in Texas or California before being allowed to travel on to places like Chicago.

Some torture survivors are officially recognized as refugees, which grants them certain legal rights and protections after they have been resettled in the United States. Refugees are defined as persons who have had to flee across an international border because of a "well-founded fear of being persecuted for reasons of race, religion, nationality, membership of a particular social group or political opinion."[5] Those who are not officially recognized as refugees, however, have a more precarious legal status when they arrive in the United States. Some have time-limited travel or work or student visas that were hastily obtained as a way to get out of their country but that will expire sooner or later. Others have false travel documents. And still others have no documents at all. They are not officially authorized to work unless they join the underground cash economy, which makes them vulnerable to exploitation by unscrupulous employers looking to take advantage of cheap labor by people who have no rights.

If they do not wish to live as undocumented persons under the radar of immigration authorities, the only path to secure legal residency is to apply for political asylum. This is a complex, emotionally demanding, and uncertain legal process that can take years.[6] Survivors must present testimony and evidence to convince skeptical immigration judges and asylum officers that they, like refugees, also have a "well-founded fear" of further persecution and harm if they should return to their homeland. Unfortunately for them, the US immigration system is an inefficient, chronically overburdened bureaucracy. There are not enough judges, asylum officers, and legal personnel to process asylum cases in a timely manner, which only prolongs the agony and suspense. In addition, asylum seekers must find their own legal representation, either by hiring a private attorney or by trying to find a pro bono attorney who will represent them for free. Language barriers, lack of money, shame, and ongoing anxiety make the entire process quite intimidating. In Chicago, the Heart-land Alliance National Immigrant Justice Center has attempted to respond to these needs by organizing a large network of volunteer attorneys who are willing to take on asylum cases for free.

There are other systemic and political obstacles encountered by desperate people seeking asylum. David Hollenbach makes note of a prevailing undercurrent of resistance and skepticism in the US immigration system about the claims of legitimate asylum seekers:

> The fact that so many people are seeking to move across bor-ders for many reasons has led to a growing resistance to admit-ting them. Concerns about national security have increased in the aftermath of September 11, 2001, and these fears mean refugees often face resistance in their efforts to obtain asylum. People moving for economic reasons are often seen as threats to the jobs and wages of people in the countries they seek to enter. Legitimate asylum seekers are sometimes seen as actu-ally in pursuit of economic advancement and thus not really owed the protection due to refugees.[7]

Regardless, and in the meantime, survivors of torture need a place to stay. The fortunate have extended family members or people from their country of origin who offer space in their homes or apartments for as long as it is needed. Others may find themselves in a variety of temporary situations, perhaps sleeping on couches or floors where they are not so sure they are welcome. The least fortunate—those who have no connections and no money—may end up homeless, eventually finding their way to homeless shelters, which are less than ideal for people suffering from post-traumatic stress because of crowding, noise, and lack of privacy.

I am moved by stories of the goodness and generosity of people who have offered sanctuary and hospitality to torture survivors dur-ing dark, inhospitable times. In Chicago, during the early 1980s, the Wellington Avenue United Church of Christ was the first among several churches to declare itself a sanctuary for Central Americans fleeing the horrific violence in their homelands. This was the era of the Reagan anti-Communist frenzy, during which the US government aided and abetted the brutal governments of El Salvador and Guatemala in counterinsurgency wars against their own people (75,000 Salvadorans were killed; 200,000 Guatemalans were killed or disappeared). For a time, these unholy alliances resulted in politically motivated blindness and resistance in the US immigration system to granting asylum or refugee status to desperate people from those countries.[8] About a decade later, as the carnage continued, two Roman Catholic sisters, Sister Pat Murphy and Sister JoAnn Persch, founded the Su Casa Catholic Worker House in Chicago as another safe place for people who had been traumatized in Central America.[9] Such places embody both meanings of the word *sanctuary*, being not only "places of refuge and protection" but also "holy places" in the truest sense of the word. The "Celtic Rune of Hospitality" comes to mind:

> I saw a stranger yesterday;
> I put food in the eating place,
> drink in the drinking place,
> music in the listening place;
> and in the sacred name of the Triune God
> he blessed myself and my house,
> my cattle and my dear ones,
> and the lark said in her song:
> Often, Often, Often,
> goes the Christ in a stranger's guise.

The point, though, is not to help survivors of torture because they might be angels in disguise (which they are) or stand-ins for Christ (which they are). We should help them simply because they are human beings who are in need of hospitality, sanctuary, and support.

TRAUMA AND RECOVERY

Judith Herman's book *Trauma and Recovery* is regarded as "the Bible" by many professionals in the field of trauma treatment. With deep insight and empathy she explores the dynamics of trauma in situations of child abuse, rape, domestic and political violence, disaster, and torture. She also lays out a useful three-phase framework for the process of healing and recovery. "The fundamental stages of recovery," she writes, "are establishing safety, reconstructing the trauma story, and restoring the connection between survivors and their community."[10] Herman writes from the vantage point of the psychotherapy relationship, but her insights are also relevant and applicable for medical professionals, lawyers, ministers, case managers, human rights workers, family members, house mates, and anyone else who has significant contact with the traumatized person.

"The work of healing begins in a safe place," writes Leston Havens.[11] The task of *establishing safety* is not only about helping survivors find refuge from actual danger but also applies to our efforts to create an emotionally safe climate in our relationship with them. In the initial stages of work with survivors, it is wise to be patient, not pressuring them to talk about traumatic experiences before they are ready to do so. We should try to follow their lead, respecting their own sense of timing about when and where and with whom they feel safe enough to tell their story. This is not always possible, especially in mental-health evaluations or legal situations where it is necessary to get detailed information about their story in order to be able to assist them. Otherwise, though, it is best to take it easy. Because interrogation and torture are characterized by coercion, disrespect, and violation of boundaries, in situations where the survivors are completely controlled and at the mercy of their torturers, it is crucial to convey respect for their sense of choice and control at all times. Even well-intentioned and sensitive inquiries about traumatic experiences can potentially recreate or reenact the interrogation situation by pushing survivors to answer questions they feel uncomfortable about and are reluctant to answer.

The first priority is anything that can be done to put survivors at ease, to help them feel safer and calmer by reducing their sense of anxiety and hyperarousal. At this stage promotion of bodily health and relaxation are more important than talking about traumatic experiences or feelings. Herman suggests that restoration of the normal biological rhythms of sleep and eating (things that most of us take for granted) is very important. If survivors are suffering from severe anxiety and insomnia, arrangements should be made as soon as possible for them to see a medical practitioner or psychiatrist who can assess whether medication for insomnia, anxiety, or depression could be helpful. With those who have lost their appetites, it is important to make sure they are eating something nourishing at regular intervals. For people who have no money to pay for food, the task is to figure out a way to get them something to eat.

One homeless torture survivor with no money was living temporarily in an old convent. He was a proud man who was embarrassed to ask for help, until he finally broke down in tears and told me that he had not eaten for three days. Another survivor who suffered from severe insomnia lived in a homeless shelter. To make matters worse, he and the other residents were getting eaten alive by bedbugs every night at the shelter. He had no place else to go and had to make the best of it. Getting him some medication for sleep and anxiety, an antihistamine to relieve itching, and some non-toxic bedbug repellant spray for his bed linens at the shelter helped to make the situation at least a little more bearable.

In the early stages of the psychotherapy or pastoral relationship with survivors, the emphasis is on support, nurture, coping, and survival. The aim is to create a supportive *holding environment*. The concept of the holding environment was developed by D. W. Winnicott, an influential British pediatrician and psychoanalyst who likened the ideal therapeutic relationship to a mother who is empathically attuned and responsive to the needs of her child at any given time. Although the holding environment is usually seen as pertaining primarily to an ambience of safety and nurture in the healing relationship, Winnicott also understood it to apply to empathic attention to issues of safety, security, stability, and routine in the day-to-day social environment of the persons for whom we are caring. With survivors' permission, it is often useful to develop collaborative connections with other important people in their lives (for example, doctors, immigration attorneys, case managers). This can help those who might otherwise fall through the cracks to feel "held," that is, cared for. Because survivors have many needs, a team approach is most effective.

Although premature exploration of trauma is unhelpful, there comes a point when survivors *need* to tell their story. Ideally, an inner emotional readiness to do so emerges naturally in its own time in the context of a trusting relationship with a professional or supportive community. Sometimes, though, external pressures or circumstances like asylum interviews or court hearings require survivors to talk about the details of their traumatic experiences in less than ideal times and circumstances. Although these can be occasions for painful re-traumatization, they are also potential opportunities for healing and empowerment. Helping survivors to prepare emotionally for telling their story to immigration officials, judges, and lawyers can help them to find their "voice" and build confidence in the legitimacy and justice of their petitions for asylum. Survivors are usually required to write their own stories of torture and persecution, which are submitted with their applications for asylum. As painful as this process can be, this reconstruction of the trauma story can help them to integrate, organize, and begin to come to terms with pains and sorrows that will forever be part of the fabric of their lives.

Cultivation of a holding environment also applies to the process of accompanying persons as they recall and recount their experiences. "As the survivor summons her memories," says Judith Herman, "the need to preserve safety must be balanced constantly against the need to face the past. . . . Avoiding the traumatic memories leads to stagnation in the recovery process, while approaching them too precipitately leads to a fruitless and damaging reliving of the trauma." Mercifully, she counsels that the process should always remain "within the realm of the bearable."[12]

Because of the nature of my work, I have often been in the privileged position of being the first person to hear the whole awful story. Although survivors feel anxiety and ambivalence about remembering and talking about what happened to them, most know on some level that they will eventually need to do so for the sake of their own healing. In her essay "Memory and Trauma," psychologist Pumla Gobodo-Madikizela reflects on this dynamic in the context of her work with the Truth and Reconciliation Commission in South Africa:

> Contrary to common protestations against revisiting the past, there is an urgency to talk about the past among many of those who have suffered gross violations of human rights. . . . The question is not whether victims will tell their stories, but whether there is an appropriate forum to express their pain.[13]

Reconstructing the trauma story is a time of *mourning and remembrance*. "The telling of the trauma story," says Herman, "inevitably plunges the survivor into profound grief."[14] The grief arises not so much as a direct result of torture but from the multiple losses that have ensued from it—beginning with a painful break from life as the person knew it before torture. Things will never be the same; the *person* will never be the same. Sometimes survivors feel as if they have died, or as if a part of themselves has died.[15] It may seem that the vital inner connection to their soul has been lost, damaged, or destroyed. Psychotherapy, in these cases, is like going on a journey to find and revive a lost soul. "The rebirth and regrowth of the lost living heart of the personality," wrote psychoanalyst Harry Guntrip, "is the ultimate problem psychotherapy now seeks to solve."[16]

Sometimes psychotherapy with survivors of torture is like accompanying them along the Via Dolorosa of their own life, walking
with them as they visit and relive the various stations along their
personal Way of Sorrows.[17] *And then they took me there. And then he
said this. . . . And then they did this . . . and that . . . and that.* This
journey is not taken for its own sake, but only if and when it seems
necessary for the sake of healing and only if survivors are able and
willing to go there. Not all of them *should* go there. Some have been
hurt more than others. Some have fewer resources than others; for
them, the work of healing should be less about revisiting the past
and more about dealing as best they can in the here and now. For
still others, though, the process of mourning and remembrance is
fruitful, redemptive, worth it.

Sooner or later, the final phase is about reconnecting to the
world, rejoining the land of the living, rebuilding a new life, moving
on. For many survivors, the moment of being granted asylum is a
personal victory or turning point that finally allows them to begin
looking ahead with less fear and a little more hope. The injustice
of their sufferings has been officially recognized, validated. They no
longer have to live in a kind of ambiguous legal limbo as immigrants
who are not sure they are really welcome. They are now authorized
to work. It is possible to begin the challenging task of creating a
more viable situation that could eventually allow for reunification
with loved ones from their homeland.

Some discover what Herman calls a "survivor mission."[18] This
can take the form of charitable service or social action on behalf
of other survivors or asylum seekers. They become *wounded healers,*
attempting to make redemptive use of their own sufferings to help
others who are in trouble. For example, Sister Dianna Ortiz, an
American missionary sister who was tortured in Guatemala, helped
to found the Torture Abolition and Survivors Support Coalition
(TASSC). She also has written a moving and harrowing memoir
of her torture and her ongoing journey of healing and recovery.[19]

VICARIOUS TRAUMA, VICARIOUS RESILIENCE

Like other professionals who have regular contact with survivors of torture, I have occasionally experienced *vicarious traumatization*, which should be considered an occupational hazard for anyone who works closely with people who have suffered severe trauma. Put simply, through the process of empathy, caregivers find themselves vicariously experiencing painful feelings that resemble the feelings of the person for whom they are caring.

I once interviewed a brave young woman who had suffered vicious racial discrimination and police brutality in her home country as punishment for her activism on behalf of basic human rights for her people. Her torture included a variety of unspeakable atrocities, including gang rape by police. As she recounted her story, I became aware of an unsettling mix of feelings in myself, beginning with a sense of profound sorrow. There was also a mounting sense of anxiety, helplessness, and horror as she recalled and relived her awful memories in my office. I found myself feeling a sense of rage toward her torturers, which was accompanied by violent fantasies of punishing them for what they had done to her. In addition, I noticed a look of anguish on the face of the language interpreter who was assisting me; she later told me that she had to go home and bathe after our session to cleanse herself of the filthy, toxic things she had just heard. I managed, for the most part, to maintain my composure and conceal my feelings behind a well-practiced professional demeanor. Afterward, though, even though it was still before noon, I felt I needed a drink—preferably some good Irish whiskey. Instead, I went down the hall to debrief with a supportive colleague—which was when my own tears started to flow. For some days afterward, haunting images of the young woman's story would come into my mind at odd times; it struck me that these resembled the kind of intrusive thoughts that often trouble people with post-traumatic stress disorder.

Another example is from a class on human rights I used to teach for idealistic, energetic college students who were preparing for immersion experiences in Latin America. After a few class sessions that required reading and watching films dealing with torture and other gross human rights violations, I noticed that many of the formerly talkative students were nearly speechless when it came time for discussion; some had markedly pained or depressed looks on their faces. There was little energy or vitality; the bottom had dropped out. The students, it seemed, were suffering from a kind of vicarious traumatization that had been triggered simply by reading and learning about the suffering of others. My slowness to recognize the distress of the students was probably a reflection of my own desensitization to trauma; I had perhaps become a little *too* used to such realities. It was necessary to step back from the traumatic and tragic to recover a sense of emotional balance, to remember the beauty and strengths and resilience of the oppressed people we were learning about.

The importance of self-care for caregivers cannot be emphasized enough. Those who work closely with traumatized and oppressed people are at especially high risk not only for vicarious traumatization in response to particular people and situations, but for emotional burnout over the long haul. Burnout is the exhausting end result of the cumulative effects of too many unprocessed feelings, too much stress, and not enough rest, support, and perspective. Breaks and vacations, time for play and relaxation, boundaries and balance between work and personal life, and meaningful relationships and interests away from work are all not only helpful but absolutely necessary if caregivers are to remain healthy and effective. Emotional and moral support from colleagues is also crucial, because we need to be able to talk with others not only about how the survivors are doing but about how *we* are doing. It is best not to do this work alone; a team approach in a supportive work environment makes it possible to share the burden of stress and responsibility rather than bearing it in isolation.

Self-awareness is also crucial, not only to detect signs of vicarious trauma or burnout in ourselves, but to avoid all kinds of unhealthy patterns that can develop in relationships with people who are in need and distress. One common response is emotional withdrawal or disengagement from people in overwhelming pain; we understandably pull away to protect ourselves from feeling too much, but in so doing we can lose the vital personal connection with a person who really needs us. On the other hand, there is also the potential for emotional overinvolvement in ways that are not only unhealthy for caregivers but unhelpful to the person we are trying to help. Finding a discerning balance between enough emotional engagement to feel connected, while also maintaining enough emotional distance to keep some objectivity and perspective, can be quite challenging and complicated. Even so, our mistakes and experiences of becoming overwhelmed are opportunities for learning to take better care of ourselves, which ultimately always helps us to serve others more effectively. For example, reflection on vicarious trauma can help us to develop empathy and insight into the world of traumatized people, because our own feelings often give us clues that can help us to appreciate and understand what they are going through. Neil Altman, a psychoanalyst who devoted a good part of his professional career to work with children and families in the South Bronx area of New York City, has written with deep insight about the therapeutic use of our own feelings in work with people in oppressive and often violent social circumstances.[20]

Finally, it is wise not only to focus on the pain and problems of torture survivors, but also to be mindful of their strengths, resources, courage, and resilience. Psychiatric perspectives, though useful, usually tend to focus almost exclusively on vulnerabilities and psychopathology. Nancy Scheper-Hughes, a medical anthropologist and scholar-activist who has devoted much of her career to understanding situations of social suffering, has advocated for a more expansive and holistic appreciation of people in situations of trauma and adversity:

The PTSD model underestimates the human capacity not only to survive, but to thrive, during and following states of emergency, extreme adversity, and everyday as well as extraordinary violence. The construction of humans as resilient and hardy or fragile, passive and easily overwhelmed by events should not be viewed as an either/or opposition. Human nature is both resilient *and* frail. There are limits to human adaptiveness. . . . But the medical-social science-psychiatric pendulum has swung in recent years toward a model of human vulnerability and human frailty to the exclusion of the awesome ability of people—adults and children—to withstand, survive, and live with horrible events.[21]

Things that help people withstand, survive, and live with horrible events include intelligence (not only "book smarts" but "street smarts"), resourcefulness, courage, perseverance, connections with supportive families and communities, and the intangible spiritual resource of faith. By faith I do not mean cognitive belief in the existence of God or participation in organized religion—though these can be very helpful too. I mean a kind of inner confidence in Someone or Something that enables and empowers a person to keep trying—*in spite of.* This is referred to in some African American churches as the Power that can make a way out of *no* way. I will never forget the time, many years ago, when a little boy was brought by his grandmother for his first appointment at a children's clinic. His mother had recently been brutally murdered in front of him, and his grandmother had stepped up to take the motherless boy into her home. She was an older African American woman who had already had a hard life even before this trauma. She was suffering from her own grief over the loss of her daughter and also having to adjust to the challenging daily responsibility of caring for a traumatized, grief-stricken little boy. Rather than focus only on the needs and problems of her grandson, though, I decided to ask her how *she* was doing with all this. "It's been rough," she said, her eyes welling up. Then she closed her eyes, as if in silent prayer, raised her hand in the air, and added, "*But God is able.*"

The generosity and courage and faith of the grandmother are awe inspiring but not unusual. Again and again I have witnessed similar resilience—even *heroism*—in my work with survivors of torture. Often, when people learn that I do this kind of work, I get comments like, "That must be so hard," or, "I don't know how you do it." I usually respond with something like, "Well, it *can* be hard to hear about terrible things, but honestly I often feel *inspired* by the people I work with. They don't drag me down; they lift me up." Many of my colleagues share this feeling, which is a good illustration of another concept in the clinical literature on work with trauma survivors: *vicarious resilience.* One group of researchers has observed: "We noticed that among the psychotherapists who work with torture survivors, some made specific reference to the inspiration and strength they drew from working with clients whom they sometimes described as 'heroes.'"[22] In spite of the emotional demands of the work, it could be said that we "catch courage" from survivors that can potentially help us to live our own lives with more bravery and integrity. The healing process goes both ways; we help them, but they help *us* too.

6

HEALING OF NATIONS

Guilt, Sorrow, and Forgiveness

Then the angel showed me the river of the water of life, bright as crystal, flowing from the throne of God and of the Lamb through the middle of the street of the city. On either side of the river is the tree of life . . . and the leaves of the tree are for the healing of the nations.
—Revelation 22:1–2

We can ask whether remembering benefits societies that have suffered trauma more than forgetting. This is not an easy question to answer, but I think it depends on how the past is remembered. If a memory is kept alive in order to kindle and cultivate old hatreds and resentments, then it is likely to culminate in vengeance. But if a memory is kept alive in order to transcend hateful emotions, to free oneself or one's society from the burden of hatred, then remembering has the power to heal.
—Pumla Gobodo-Madikizela[1]

HEALING IS NOT only a personal, individual matter for the hearts and minds and souls of individual survivors of trauma. It also has collective dimensions; traumatized communities and nations are sorely in need of healing too. "Remembering and telling the truth about terrible events," writes Judith Herman, "are prerequisites both for the restoration of the social order and for the healing of individual victims."[2] Societies torn apart by destructive violence and widespread violations of human rights can be crippled by unhealed wounds, unforgiven sins, unpunished crimes, unmourned losses. If some measure of reconciliation and restoration of the social order are to be possible, painful truths must be acknowledged, parties responsible for harm must be held accountable, and processes of repentance and mourning must be allowed to run their natural course.

In this chapter I explore the complex and demanding process of communal recovery for societies that have suffered social catastrophes. I begin with some reflections on communities that have suffered massive historical trauma, focusing in particular on the Lakota people of North America. Then I explore some examples of ways particular nations have attempted to come to terms with their trauma in different contexts: the Recovery of Historical Memory Project in Guatemala, and the Truth and Reconciliation Commission in South Africa.

TO DIE AND COME BACK

In the Lakota Sioux language, the word *takini* means "one who has been brought back to life"[3] or "to die and come back."[4] It is usually translated more simply as "survivor," but the other meanings have deeper and richer spiritual resonances.

For the Lakota, a collective sense of death and traumatic grief is particularly associated with the massacre of as many as three hundred Lakota men, women, and children by the US Seventh Cavalry at Wounded Knee Creek on December 29, 1890. The bodies were thrown into a mass grave. After decades of relentless encroachment and assaults by white settlers and the US military, the Lakota experienced Wounded Knee as the final, annihilating, genocidal deathblow to their people and culture.

Black Elk, a witness to Wounded Knee, was a Lakota holy man and healer whose long life [1862–1950] spanned the waning days of the great Sioux buffalo hunting culture, through the bitter battles with the US military over the Black Hills and the Great Plains, to their inevitable defeat and the near-total destruction of their culture by forced confinement on Indian reservations. He lived out the last sixty or so years of his life not far from Wounded Knee on the Pine Ridge Reservation. He eventually converted to Catholicism through the Jesuit missionaries at Pine Ridge, but he also always preserved and practiced the older Lakota spirituality and healing traditions. As an old man Black Elk recalled what went through his mind as he surveyed the grim aftermath of the massacre:

> And so it was all over. I did not know then how much was ended. When I look back now from this high hill of my old age, I can still see the butchered women and children lying heaped and scattered all along the crooked gulch as plain as when I saw them with eyes still young. And I can see that something else died there in the bloody mud, and was buried in the blizzard. A people's dream died there. It was a beautiful dream.[5]

"This massacre has reverberated through the hearts and minds of Lakota survivors and descendants," writes Dr. Maria Yellow Horse Brave Heart, who is herself a descendant of survivors of Wounded Knee.[6] At one point in her life, Brave Heart recognized that she was carrying a grief that she described as being "bigger than myself." She began to reflect on the impact of massive group trauma, not only upon the direct victims and survivors, but also on their children and grandchildren and generations of future descendants. In 1992 she founded the Takini Network, a nonprofit organization devoted to community healing among the Lakota and other Native peoples.

As a clinical social worker and researcher, Brave Heart developed the concepts of *historical trauma* and *unresolved historical grief* and

applied them to her own people. Pathological manifestations of
the historical trauma response among the Lakota include rampant
depression, alcoholism, injuries and deaths from alcohol-related
car accidents, domestic violence, child abuse, homicide, suicide,
unemployment, and poor physical health. The Pine Ridge Indian
Reservation, where the Wounded Knee massacre site can be found,
is located in Shannon County, South Dakota, which has the unfortunate and long-time distinction of being one of the poorest
counties in the United States.

Drawing on the writings of Robert Jay Lifton on trauma and
death, and also on the psychological literature on multi-generational
transmission of trauma in Jewish Holocaust survivors and their descendants, Brave Heart theorizes that one of the deeper underlying
dynamics of the historical trauma response among the Lakota is
"identification with the dead, so that one feels psychically (emotionally and psychologically) dead and feels unworthy of living."[7]
This pervasive sense of numbness and death is a central feature
of the experience of communities that survive (barely) without a
sense of vitality and dignity and worth—that go on existing after
the dream has died.

Lifton theorizes that survivors of massive trauma and death
sometimes form what he calls an "identity of the dead." In some
cases—for example, survivors of the US atomic bomb attacks on
Japan or inmates of the Nazi concentration camps—they may
experience themselves as if they *are* dead.[8] For his book *Death in
Life*, Lifton interviewed survivors of the US atomic bomb attack
on Hiroshima, who are known in Japan as *hibakusha*, "those who
were bombed." On August 6, 1945, at the moment of the explosion,
66,000 residents of that city were incinerated instantly; as many as
200,000 died from bomb-related injuries and radiation sickness by
1950 (not including another 140,000 in Nagasaki). It is understand-
able that survivors of such an atrocity resort to psychic numbing,
a diminished capacity to feel, as a way to cope with an unbearable

death-filled world and with the unbearable feelings and memories
of it that they carry within themselves.

In extreme cases some survivors take on the appearance of "living
corpses" or "walking ghosts."[9] Primo Levi, an Italian Jewish chemist
who became one of the great literary witnesses of the Holocaust,
describes such persons as "non-men who march and labor in silence,
the divine spark dead within them, already too empty to suffer.
One hesitates to call them living: one hesitates to call their death
death."[10] Something analogous to the "divine spark" is known in
Jewish mysticism as the *shekinah,* the "indwelling presence" of God
in the world, a spirit that also dwells within the soul of each human
person.[11] Elie Wiesel, in profound despair and disillusionment after
the harrowing experience of the Nazi camps, writes, "We . . . lived
with the illusion that every one of us had been entrusted with a
sacred spark from the shekinah's flame; that every one of us carries
in his eyes and his soul a reflection of God's image."[12] How heartbreaking to witness the extinguishing of the divine spark within the
human soul, to see the light go out in people's eyes, to watch help-
lessly as this happens to oneself! The words of Jeremiah are fitting:

> For the hurt of my poor people I am hurt,
> I mourn, and dismay has taken hold of me.
> Is there no balm in Gilead? Is there no physician
>   there?
> Why then has the health of my poor people not
>   been restored?
> O that my head were a spring of water, and my
>   eyes a fountain of tears,
> So that I might weep day and night
> for the slain of my poor people! (Jer 8:22—9:1)

But is there really no balm in Gilead? Is the divine spark actually
dead? Is there no way for crucified peoples to come back to the

land of the living? As an old man, after many decades of reservation life, Black Elk continued to feel a deep and persistent sense of grief and dismay about the plight of his people. A moving passage from *Black Elk Speaks* recounts a climb he made to the top of Harney Peak in the Black Hills, a place that had once been revealed to him as "the center of the world" in a childhood vision. There, looking over the remarkable landscape so sacred to the Lakota, the sorrowful old man lamented and prayed for some inkling of hope and possibility for them. He recalled an image of a lush, beautiful tree from his childhood vision, a tree meant to bloom with all the hopes and dreams of his people:

> Grandfather, Great Spirit, once more behold me on earth and lean to hear my feeble voice. . . . Today I send a voice for a people in despair. . . . With tears running . . . I must say now that the tree has never bloomed. A pitiful old man, you see me here, and I have fallen away and done nothing. Here at the center of the world, where you took me when I was young and taught me; here, old, I stand, and the tree is withered, Grandfather, my Grandfather! Again, and maybe the last time on this earth, I recall the vision you sent me. It may be that some little root of the sacred tree still lives. Nourish it then, that it may leaf and bloom and fill with singing birds. Hear me, not for myself, but for my people; I am old. . . . Hear me in my sorrow, for I may never call again. O make my people live![13]

RECOVERY OF HISTORICAL MEMORY

"Even remembering this makes you want to cry," said the person identified only as *Case 6102, Barrillas, Huehuetenango, 1982.* "You really feel what the people felt."[14]

Case 6102 is one of thousands of personal testimonies of witnesses and survivors of human rights violations that were collected by the Recovery of Historical Memory Project (REMHI), a unique pastoral initiative of the Human Rights Office of the Archdiocese of Guatemala. The project involved careful, sensitive interviews with survivors of the war, the majority of whom were impoverished Mayan people from the highland areas of the country (places like Barillas, Huehuetenango). The goal was not only to collect data, but also to offer traumatized peoples and communities the opportunity to tell their stories, to talk about what they had seen and experienced, so that their grief and suffering could be heard, honored, remembered.

The thirty-six year war (1960–96), known simply as *la Violencia* to the people, claimed over 200,000 lives, including more than 50,000 people who were "disappeared" and never seen again. The violence reached demonic proportions during a succession of vicious military dictatorships in the late 1970s and early 1980s: hundreds of massacres and thousands of extrajudicial executions of innocent civilians by the Guatemalan Army and its agents (many buried in mass graves or clandestine cemeteries), a scorched-earth counterinsurgency policy of destroying entire villages in Mayan areas, and systematic use of sadistic torture and rape to humiliate and punish and terrorize entire communities. REMHI confirmed what was already known—that the Guatemalan government and military were responsible for the great majority of these gross violations of human rights.

The findings of REMHI were largely mirrored in the 1999 report of the Commission for Historical Clarification (CEH), which was mandated by the United Nations–brokered Peace Accords. The CEH assigned responsibility for 93 percent of all human rights violations to government-sponsored military and paramilitary forces. CEH documented 626 massacres and the complete destruction of over four hundred Mayan villages. Soldiers would surround villages and then abuse, rape, torture, and murder the population "through spectacles of violence that sometimes lasted for several days."[15] Significantly, CEH also found that the state carried out a deliberate policy of genocide against the Mayan population in certain areas of the country. The CEH also examined the historical and structural roots of *la Violencia* in Guatemala's severe poverty, racism against the indigenous Mayan people, and profound inequality of the Guatemalan political and economic system, which has been dominated by a small, military-backed elite that has controlled the country's land and wealth since the colonial era. Even now, 50 percent of the Guatemalan people live in poverty, with 15 percent in extreme poverty. Forty percent of children under five years old are chronically malnourished. Figures are even worse for the Mayan people; over 75 percent live in poverty, with at least 25 percent in extreme poverty.[16]

REMHI was presided over by Monseñor Juan José Gerardi Conedera, the bishop who headed the Human Rights Office. As the final report of its findings was being edited and prepared for release, Gerardi told one of his colleagues that he wanted a report that would "enter readers through their pores" and *move* them.[17] The mandate of the CEH did not allow for individualizing responsibility and identification of perpetrators by name (thus conferring a kind of general amnesty). Gerardi, however, was appalled by the official culture of lies and silence and impunity for outrageous crimes, and he wanted REMHI, as much as possible, to *name names*—not only of victims but of *perpetrators* of the violence (individuals, commanders, military units, and so forth).

Because Gerardi had served as bishop for some of the areas of the country most traumatized by the war (Verapaz and Quiché), he had personally witnessed some of the carnage, which included the murders of hundreds of church workers (lay leaders, catechists, nuns, and priests), whose care for the poor was viewed as "subversive" by the authorities. At one point, in fear and in protest, Gerardi made the controversial decision to *close* the diocese of Quiché because the atmosphere was so deadly and dangerous (the CEH determined that the behavior of the Army in the department of Quiché met the criteria for genocide). He narrowly escaped an Army ambush in 1980, the same year Central American bishop Oscar Romero was assassinated. Later that same year, after a trip to the Vatican, the government refused to allow Gerardi to reenter Guatemala, causing him to go into exile for two years in Costa Rica. All these things deepened his sense of solidarity and identification with the abused poor of Guatemala, whom he increasingly came to regard as the living embodiment of the tortured Christ. "The suffering of Christ in his mystical body," he said, "is something that should cause us to reflect; that is to say, if the poor are out of our lives, then, maybe, Christ is out of our lives."[18]

On April 24, 1998, at a speech marking the occasion at the Metropolitan Cathedral in Guatemala City, Monseñor Gerardi publicly released the four-volume REMHI report, *Guatemala, Nunca Mas!* (Guatemala, never again!). The final volume, *Victimas del Conflicto* (victims of the conflict), contains the names of 52,427 victims of extrajudicial murder, massacres, rape, torture, disappearance, and deaths that resulted from persecution (hunger, exposure, lack of medical treatment for displaced and injured people—at the heights of the violence as many as 1.5 million people were either internally displaced or had fled the country to Mexico or the United States). Although some perpetrators are identified, care was taken to mask the identity of others in the interests of protecting survivors and their communities from reprisals.

Gerardi's words on the occasion of the release of the report were stirring; they offer not only a deeper understanding of REMHI but a glimpse into the soul of the man:

> The REMHI project is a legitimate and painful denunciation that we must listen to with profound respect and a spirit of solidarity. . . . When we began this project, we were interested in discovering the truth in order to share it. We were interested in reconstructing the history of pain and death, understanding the reasons for it, the why and the how. We sought to show the human drama and to share with others the sorrow and anguish

of the thousands of the dead, disappeared, and tortured. . . . We are collecting the people's memories because we want to contribute to the construction of a different country. The path was and continues to be full of risks, but the construction of the Kingdom of God entails risks, and only those who have the strength to confront those risks can be its builders. . . .

Years of terror and death have . . . reduced the majority of Guatemalans to fear and silence. *Truth* is the primary word, the serious and mature action that makes it possible for us to break this cycle of death and violence and to open ourselves to a future of hope and light for all. REMHI's work has been an astonishing endeavor of discovery, exploration, and appropriation of our personal and collective history. It has been an open door for people to breathe and speak in freedom and for the creation of communities with hope. Peace is possible—a peace born from the truth that comes from each one of us and from all of us. It is a painful truth, full of memories of the country's deep and bloody wounds. It is a liberating and humanizing truth that makes it possible for men and women to come to terms with themselves and their life stories. It is a truth that challenges each one of us to recognize our individual and collective responsibility and to commit ourselves to action so that those abominable acts never happen again.[19]

Gerardi, at age seventy-five, felt a sense of relief and accomplishment at having shepherded the REMHI project to its completion. He joked about finally slowing down and considering retirement. Nonetheless, this was Guatemala, and he was acutely aware that "the path was and continues to be full of risks." Despite his playful persona (he had a reputation as a *chistoso* or jokester), friends and colleagues from the Human Rights Office noted his anxiety and preoccupation with the possibility of retaliation from those whose criminality was exposed in the REMHI report. He encouraged his staff members to be vigilant and to take extra precautions for themselves and their families, to look into options for study abroad, to take a long trip out of the country.

On April 26, 1998, two days after the release of the REMHI report, Gerardi took his car from the garage of the San Sebastian Parish rectory where he lived in Guatemala City and went out for dinner with his sister. Upon his return later that evening, he was bludgeoned to death with a concrete slab by a team of assassins in his garage. His heartbroken colleagues and allies and friends assembled at the gruesome crime scene, immediately suspicious that the killing was a vindictive reprisal from authorities who wished to punish and silence Gerardi for his audacity—and thereby frighten anyone else who might follow his example.

Francisco Goldman, a prize-winning Guatemalan American author who happened to have been baptized at the Church of San Sebastian where Monseñor Gerardi lived, found himself intensely interested in the unfolding of the murder investigation. Though he was primarily a fiction writer, Goldman soon embarked on what turned out to be seven years of demanding investigative journalism, including his own detective work, to document the dramatic, dangerous, and often bizarre unfolding of the case that became known as Guatemala's "crime of the century." The result was his magnificent and disturbing 2007 book *The Art of Political Murder: Who Killed the Bishop?*[20]

The book gives a palpable feel for postwar Guatemala, especially the scary, poverty-stricken, crime-ridden reality of Guatemala City. It reads like a suspense-filled detective novel, with many odd twists and turns, shady characters, and unsung heroes. Perhaps most inspiring are the members of Monseñor Gerardi's staff at the Human Rights Office, who, because of their many disappointing experiences with the Guatemalan judicial system, decided to embark upon their own parallel investigation to get to the bottom of who was responsible for the killing of their beloved friend and mentor. This included a group of remarkable young men known as *los Intocables* (the untouchables), so named because their relentless and fearless pursuit of truth and justice were reminiscent of Elliott Ness and his companions in their pursuit of Al Capone and his murderous organized crime network in Chicago in the 1920s. The analogy is apt not only for *los Intocables,* but for the notoriously corrupt and violent institutional culture of the military, intelligence, police, and government systems in Guatemala, which have often been likened to an elaborate network of organized crime.

Beyond the daunting task of identifying and prosecuting Gerardi's killers, the bigger issue was the battle against the official culture of impunity in Guatemala, which was summed up succinctly in one of the testimonies for the CEH: "I feel that the most difficult thing in Guatemala is to see that so much injustice has been committed and, yet, it goes completely unpunished. Everything is as it was. No one can do anything. I feel that the murderers, the oppressors that are in the country continue living undisturbed. That is what is most difficult to accept."[21]

Eventually, remarkably, after an arduous investigation and a dramatic trial during which prosecuting attorneys and judges were threatened (including hand grenades thrown into the backyard of one of the judges), and witnesses intimidated or killed under questionable circumstances, three army officers (along with a priest who may have been an accomplice in tracing Gerardi's movements and tampering with evidence) were tried and convicted in a civilian court in June 2001. The officers—Colonel Byron Lima Estrada; his son, Captain Byron Lima Oliva; and Sergeant Major Obdulio Villanueva—were sentenced to thirty years in prison for their part in the conspiracy to murder Monseñor Gerardi; the priest, Mario Orantes, was sentenced to twenty years. Although the thirty-year sentences were later reduced to twenty years, and though the Human Rights Office and others were frustrated that evidence that might lead to the higher-level "intellectual authors" of the crime was never pursued, the verdicts were nonetheless celebrated as a major victory in the battle against impunity in Guatemala.

The path, however, continued to be full of risks. In January 2006, during a court appeal by the convicted army officers, the tortured and mutilated corpse of Darinel Domingo, the younger brother of the lead attorney for the Human Rights Office, Mario Domingo, was found in Guatemala City. One of his limbs had been torn off.

One of the leads that was never officially pursued was the testimony of a key witness that implicated the current president of Guatemala, General Otto Pérez Molina, in the Gerardi murder. On the night of the crime the witness had observed General Pérez Molina, who served as the director of Military Intelligence in the 1990s, talking to Colonel Lima Estrada in a bodega just a few blocks away from Gerardi's residence. The Human Rights Office and the prosecution believe that the officers were there to monitor and supervise the crime.[22]

There have been other important challenges to the culture of impunity in Guatemala. Most recently, in May 2013, General Efrain Rios Montt, the eighty-six-year-old former dictator, was convicted of genocide. Specifically, he was found guilty of ordering the murders of 1,771 Ixil Maya people (a small fraction of all those actually killed during his seventeen-month reign of terror in 1982–83). Though the verdict was soon overturned because of legal complications, the fact that the trial even occurred was widely regarded as another major breakthrough for justice and accountability in Guatemala.

Significantly, during the Rios Montt trial, evidence emerged that also implicated the current president of the country, Otto Pérez Molina, in genocidal massacres committed against the Mayan people during the war. Hugo Reyes, a former soldier who served under the command of Pérez Molina, gave the following testimony:

> The soldiers, on orders from Major "Tito Arias," better known as Otto Pérez Molina . . . coordinated the looting and burning, in order to later execute people. . . . The people who were to

be executed arrived at the camp beaten, tortured, their tongues cut out, their fingernails pulled out.[23]

It remains to be seen whether evidence linking Perez Molina not only to the Gerardi murder, but to the greater crime of mass murder during the war, will ever be pursued. To the shame of the United States, the major players in both the Gerardi murder and the genocide were trained at the School of the Americas, whose graduates include Colonel Lima Estrada, General Pérez Molina, and General Rios Montt.

Monseñor Gerardi, to be sure, would be pleased and proud of all these developments, which are not just about holding tyrants accountable, but about remembering and honoring the victims. "Breaking through our amnesia, remembering the victims, has a double effect," writes Elizabeth Johnson:

> First, by keeping alive their story against the inclination of tyrants to bury it, it robs the masters of their victory. History is written by the victors, who strut about as if the dead over whom they climbed did not count. But memory keeps the reality of their lives alive, in protest against their defeat and in commitment to their unfinished agenda. Second, by connecting their story to the story of Jesus, memory awakens the realization that each one of them is precious, galvanizing hope that in God's good time they too will be justified. What there is at present, the victory of those who murder and harm, is not the last word.[24]

TRUTH AND RECONCILIATION

Not long after fall of the racist apartheid regime in South Africa with the election of President Nelson Mandela in 1994, it became clear to the new leadership that something needed to be done to facilitate healing and reconciliation in the traumatized nation. Mandela appointed Anglican Archbishop Desmond Tutu to preside over what would become known as the Truth and Reconciliation Commission (TRC). Tutu's memoir, *No Future Without Forgiveness,* offers a moving, firsthand account of the dramatic and remarkable unfolding of the process of a nation attempting to confront its painful past and grapple with the truth of its own deep wounds and bitter divisions.[25] In the words of Judge Ismail Mahomed, Chief Justice of South Africa during the era of the TRC, the nation needed to come to terms with "the truth of wounded memories."[26]

The hearings of the TRC were convened on April 15, 1996, and were held regularly for over two years until they were formally closed on July 31, 1998. Victims of gross human rights violations during the apartheid regime were invited to tell their stories at public TRC hearings. There were plenty of stories to tell, because the white supremacist apartheid regime had maintained itself in power from 1948 to 1994 through the systematic practice of murder, torture, violent repression of dissent, and blatant racist segregation. Over twenty thousand statements were taken from victims of human rights violations and their families. In addition, over seven thousand perpetrators of politically motivated human rights violations petitioned the TRC for amnesty from prosecution for their crimes under certain conditions, including publicly telling the whole truth about what they had done.

On a personal level, the TRC hearings were often an emotionally wrenching experience for Tutu. On the second day of the packed hearings in East London, an older man by the name of Singqokwana Malgas was scheduled to testify. Mr. Malgas was a member of the African National Congress who had spent fourteen years of his life with other black political prisoners at the infamous Robben Island prison. He had been brutally tortured numerous times by South African security forces. His home had been burned down, and his son Simphiwe had been tortured to death with acid by the police in 1985. He had suffered a stroke that affected his speech and left him partially paralyzed, and so he was wheeled into the hearings in a wheelchair. Tutu recalls:

Mr. Malgas tried to describe some of the torture methods used on him. He began to speak about one that we were to encounter many times afterward—the so-called "helicopter" method. The police handcuff your hands behind your back, your ankles are manacled together, then you are suspended upside down and spun around. Mr. Malgas tried to elaborate on his written statement and tell us all this. Whether it was that he could not bear to recall the memories of the torture or whether he was frustrated that his tongue could not articulate what he wanted to tell us I will never know. . . . Whatever the reason, he just put his normal hand over his face and cried. I was too full from all that I had heard and it was all too much for me too. I just broke down and sobbed like a child. The floodgates opened. I bent over the table and covered my face with my hands. I told people afterward that I laugh easily and cry easily and wondered whether I was the right person to lead the commission since I knew I was so weak and vulnerable.[27]

Tutu resolved to make every effort to control his emotions and maintain his composure in future hearings, so as not to divert attention away from those who were there to tell their stories. Nonetheless, his genuineness and spontaneity frequently brought a tone of personal warmth and compassion to situations that might otherwise have taken on a more legalistic, courtroom style. For example, at one hearing the widow of an anti-apartheid activist who had been tortured and murdered broke into a piercing, agonized wail. "In many ways," said Tutu, "her cry was the defining sound of the TRC—as a place where people could come to cry, to open their hearts, to expose the anguish that had remained locked up for so long, unacknowledged, ignored, and denied. I adjourned the proceedings so that she could recover her composure and when we restarted, I led the gathering in singing "Senzenina [What Have We Done?]."[28]

> What have we done?
> Our sin is that we are black?
> Our sin is the truth.
> They are killing us.
> Let Africa return.

Tutu and the TRC leadership were attempting to manage and steer an ambitious, unwieldy, public therapeutic process with deeply traumatized people and communities. The process was not without tension and controversy, both behind the scenes within the TRC leadership and in the country at large. The emotional nature of the hearings gave rise to the TRC being labeled by some the Kleenex Commission. Sometimes hearings were contentious and unpredictable. For example, at one packed amnesty hearing in Bisho, the site of a 1992 massacre of twenty-eight demonstrators by soldiers, the crowd became incensed and hostile in response to the controlled, unemotional testimony of one of the white generals responsible for the troops. The tone changed completely, however, when another witness, a white officer named Horst Shobesberger, made the following appeal:

> "I say we are sorry. I say the burden of the Bisho massacre will be on our shoulders the rest of our lives. We cannot wish it away. It happened. But please, I ask specifically the victims not to forget, I cannot ask this, but to forgive us, to get the soldiers back into the community, to accept them fully, to try to understand also the pressure they were under then. This is all I can do. I'm sorry, this I can say, I'm sorry."[29]

The crowd, which to that point had been enraged and on the verge of violence, broke into thunderous *applause*. When the applause died down, Tutu marked the powerful moment by saying: "Can we just keep a moment's silence, please, because we are dealing with things that are very, very deep. It isn't easy, as we all know, to ask for forgiveness and it's also not easy to forgive, but we are people who know that when someone cannot be forgiven there is no future."[30]

Complex questions related to amnesty, accountability, and forgiveness for perpetrators of human rights violations were the most controversial and divisive aspect of the TRC process. Many amnesty applications were granted by the TRC, but some were denied, including those of five security branch officers who had participated in the murder of Black Consciousness leader Steven Biko in 1977. (Among other concerns, the TRC questioned the full truthfulness of the petitioners in their disclosures about how Biko died.)

Many daunting and emotionally charged questions arose. Is the language of apology and forgiveness even appropriate in dealing with gross human rights violations and unspeakable atrocities? Is it just or fair for perpetrators to be allowed to go free and move on with their lives without punishment or legal consequences for their crimes? What are the limits of forgiveness? How does one judge the genuineness or sincerity of a perpetrator's remorse or apology? Is forgiveness possible without justice, or when human rights violators do not take responsibility for their crimes? Is reconciliation even possible between peoples who have disliked, mistrusted, and even despised each other for generations? These complex questions are beyond the scope of this book, but they merit vigorous debate and careful discernment within the unique social context and history of any given case or situation.[31]

Pumla Gobodo-Madikizela, a South African psychologist who served on the TRC's Human Rights Violations Committee, wrestles deeply with these questions of accountability and forgiveness on both professional and personal levels in *A Human Being Died That Night: A South African Woman Confronts the Legacy of Apartheid*.[32] Most poignant and unsettling are her accounts of her visits and conversations with Eugene de Cock, the commanding officer of the notorious Vlakplaas torture and death squad unit, who was serving a life sentence for his crimes at the Pretoria Central Prison. Rather than dismissing him outright as a hopeless psychopath, she portrays de Cock with remarkable depth and complexity as a man struggling with his own uneasy conscience over a multitude of sins. Whether in personal dialogue with individual perpetrators like de Cock, or in the public forum of TRC hearings, Gobodo-Madikizela argues with considerable personal authority that "sustained, engaged, ordered dialogue . . . forces an offender to unearth what moral sensibilities he has buried under a façade of 'obedience to orders' or righteous 'duty to country' not in the heady climate of the period of mayhem but in the sobering atmosphere of reflection on ordinary lives now shattered."[33] Throughout, she is careful to make a distinction between *understanding* perpetrators and *condoning* their actions. She sees humane understanding and just treatment of offenders as a crucial component of the national reconciliation process.

Though the TRC hearings were formally closed in 1998, deep and widespread needs for healing and reconciliation in South Africa persist. One effort to respond to these needs has been the Institute for Healing of Memories in Cape Town, one of the founding members of which was Father Michael Lapsley. An Anglican priest from New Zealand, Lapsley first came to South Africa in 1973 and quickly found himself caught up in the struggle against apartheid. His outspoken criticisms of racism and violent repression resulted in his expulsion from the country in 1976. Lapsley's commitment to the anti-apartheid struggle continued from exile in Lesotho and, later, Zimbabwe.

In 1990, in retaliation for his ongoing support for resistance to the apartheid regime, Lapsley was severely injured by a letter bomb sent to him by South African security forces; the explosion blew off both of his hands and caused him to lose one of his eyes. After a long convalescence, and with the fall of the apartheid government, Lapsley returned to South Africa to continue his priestly ministry, which eventually evolved into his work with the Institute for Healing of Memories, which now offers workshops and programs not only in South Africa but in other strife-torn areas of the world.

Lapsley is a beautiful example of a *wounded healer*; he has found a way to make use of his own sufferings to facilitate the process of healing in others. His remarkable story is told in the book *Redeeming the Past: My Journey from Freedom Fighter to Healer.*[34]

7

GLIMPSES OF REDEMPTON

Threatened with Resurrection

It isn't the noise in the streets
that keeps us from resting, my friend. . . .
It is something within us that doesn't let us sleep,
that doesn't let us rest,
that won't stop pounding, deep inside.
It is the silent, warm weeping
of Indian women without their husbands.
It is the sad gaze of the children
fixed somewhere beyond memory,
precious in our eyes. . . .
What keeps us from sleeping
is that they have threatened us
with Resurrection!
 —Julia Esquivel[1]

They whisper around to me that my life has been in vain
They do not know that so wounded I am more awake.
 —Mak Dizdar[2]

IT MAY SEEM strange to look for signs of hope amid the human wreckage of torture. Yet the peculiar intuition at the heart of the spirituality of the cross is that it is the tortured one who is mysteriously able to heal us, liberate us, *save* us. The tortured one comes back to life, rises again, and, in so doing, helps others to do the same. "One has to be a little mad, kind of crazy," writes James Cone, "to find salvation in the cross, victory in defeat, and life in death."[3]

In a little essay titled "Learning to Live" Thomas Merton offers some thoughts on how our individual salvation is integrally bound up with our participation in a wider process of healing and redemption of the world in which we live.[4] This is why it sometimes feels as if our very souls are at stake when we are wrestling with our callings in important matters of love or work or conscience. They are! Not just in the sense that decisions made during our earthly lifetime affect our prospects for salvation in the world to come, but in terms of the precious opportunity we are given to save our integrity and dignity and humanity in *this* life by discovering who we are, what we have to offer, where we stand on the important issues of our time, how we can help.[5] As Merton sees it, the point of all learning—in school and in life—is to wake up, to come alive, to learn what is required to save our souls while we have the chance. The task is

> to help men and women to save their souls and, in so doing, to save their society. From what? From the hell of meaninglessness, of obsession, of complex artifice, of systematic lying, of criminal evasions and neglects, of self-destructive futilities. . . . Education in this sense, means more than learning; and for such education, one is awarded no degree. One graduates by rising from the dead.[6]

The kind of resurrection he is talking about, I think, is a process that potentially begins right here, right now, for each of us, while we are alive.

This concluding chapter is a meditation on rising from the dead. I begin with a story of a young interrogator at Abu Ghraib who experienced a profound, life-changing awakening of conscience in the bleak reality of that horrible place. All of us, though—whoever and wherever we are—are called to wake up and become more deeply human. Jon Sobrino refers to this as "awakening from the sleep of inhumanity."[7] The most awesome examples of this are crucified people who rise from the dead.

LETTERS FROM ABU GHRAIB

A few years ago I got in the car and drove from Chicago out beyond the Mississippi River to Iowa City, Iowa, where I interviewed a young Iraq veteran named Joshua Casteel. I knew a little of his story and had seen a YouTube video of him titled "How I Became a Conscientious Objector," which had made me want to hear more about how his remarkable life had unfolded. His book, *Letters from Abu Ghraib,* had recently been published.[8] The book consists of Joshua's emails to family and friends during a period of intense inner crisis while he was serving as a US Army interrogator at Abu Ghraib prison in Iraq.[9]

At the time I met him, Joshua was a graduate student in a program in nonfiction writing and playwriting at the University of Iowa. We arranged to meet at a little coffee place near the university. He made a striking appearance—a handsome, broad-shouldered guy in his late twenties who had been a football star in his high school days. He sported a small goatee, which offered a touch of rakish contrast to his Middle American good looks and military background. After a cup of coffee, we headed off to a room at a local library where I could turn on my digital recorder for the actual interview.

Joshua had grown up in an Evangelical Christian, Republican, military family. His dad had been an Army captain; an aunt had been in the service; and his grandfather had served in World War II, Korea, and Vietnam. "I grew up as a nationalist Christian," he explained. "Being a Christian was synonymous with being an American." Though he later made a radical break with this uncritical mix of faith and patriotism, for most of his childhood and adolescence it was unquestioned. "It was a very provincial sort of Christianity, intensely patriotic. . . . You served God by serving country." He enlisted in the Army Reserves at seventeen, and it seemed only natural that he would be off to the US Military Academy at West Point after high school graduation.

At West Point, though, doubts began to surface about the moral rigidity and conformity of military culture. He recalled his boot camp exercises: "The drill sergeant would say, 'What's the spirit of the bayonet?' And we'd respond, 'Kill, kill, kill without mercy, sergeant!' And he'd say, 'What makes the green grass grow?' And we'd say, 'Blood, blood, bright red blood, sergeant!'" Joshua left West Point after just three months, landing at the University of Iowa on an ROTC scholarship. During college, he struggled with depression and increasing uneasiness about the direction of his life. "I found myself being different. I wasn't seeing things the way other people were seeing things." He became preoccupied with deep questions about meaning and suffering that didn't seem to be adequately dealt with by the religion of his upbringing.

"Suffering was the key," he explained. "I couldn't understand why we always had to be happy in church, why everything was about victory. There was this need to get rid of pain and suffering. You can't avoid suffering! I couldn't sit through evangelical services. I was way too depressed to have to deal with tambourines! I mean, the key moment of Christian history was a moment of torture, of execution." He began to attend Anglican services; later he became a Catholic. "The solace of Catholicism for me," he explained, "is that the body of Christ is still on the cross."

During college Joshua also allowed himself to think beyond the provincial politics of his upbringing. In the 2000 presidential elections he voted for a non-Republican for the first time. Doing so, for him, was a considerable spiritual risk. "In Bush versus Gore, I voted for Al Gore," he laughed, "and I thought I might go to hell for it! I mean, in high school I had been the president of the Young Republicans! But I just couldn't bring myself to vote for Bush."

Then came the 9/11 terrorist attacks. Although he had qualms about the so-called War on Terror, Joshua felt a duty to reenlist, which he did after graduating from the University of Iowa in 2002. After being sent to military language school to study Arabic, he was assigned as an interrogator and Arabic linguist to the Army's 202nd Military Intelligence Battalion at the Joint Interrogation and Debriefing Center at Abu Ghraib prison in Iraq. At that time, in June 2004, the White House and the Pentagon were in major "clean up" and "damage control" mode. Just one month before, the scandalous photos of Iraqi prisoners being tortured and humiliated at Abu Ghraib had been made public.

Although Joshua said he did not observe or participate in torture or maltreatment of prisoners at Abu Ghraib, he began to have profound misgivings about the US mission in Iraq and his own role in it. He eventually conducted about 140 interrogations but found himself disgusted that the great majority of those he interrogated were obviously innocent of any wrongdoing. "I can count on one hand the people who were guilty of anything worse than being an Arab," he said. "These were young fathers, local laborers, imams, veterans of previous wars, taxi drivers—*not* terrorists, *not* insurgents. I once had to interrogate a fourteen-year-old boy who was terrified because he was missing his school exams!" In addition, the security situation was precarious; insurgents from the surrounding area would regularly attack the Abu Ghraib complex with mortars, and convoys of US personnel coming to or from the prison were frequently ambushed by snipers and roadside bombs. Joshua admitted that he was still suffering from some persisting PTSD symptoms from his Iraq experience.

Joshua experienced a mounting sense of anxiety, confusion, and inner conflict over his first few months at Abu Ghraib, which he attempted to cope with through prayer and spiritual reading. When he wasn't in the interrogation room, he could be found either in the chapel or reading books by Thomas Merton, Dorothy Day, Henri Nouwen, and Dietrich Bonhoeffer. (He once read *The Cost of Discipleship* in the interrogation room as he waited for a prisoner to be delivered.) The sense of contradiction and hypocrisy was almost unbearable. "There was a period of time when I couldn't even pray. I was such a contradiction! Either I had to stop doing what I was doing, or I had to stop praying—I couldn't do both at the same time. I couldn't interrogate poor people, I couldn't harass poor people and pray the *Magnificat* at the same time." His sense of agitation and anger is apparent in emails he sent to family and friends: "I'm simply livid. I walk around the prison so often wanting to hit things, or scream." Or, "This morning I awoke wrecked by anxiety. For a full two hours I could not move. All I could think of was failure, contradiction, falsity."[10]

In a poignant email to his father on October 10, 2004, it is clear that Joshua was in a deep state of moral crisis that was nearing the point of no return:

> I am absolutely convinced that service in my current way is absolutely wrong, and totally outside the bounds of the New Testament. If people do not understand . . . and think me a deserter, so be it. . . . I'm not at the end of my road yet on what exactly my conviction of a call to discipleship means. But I will take deadly serious Christ's call to Peter that he drop his nets and follow. I cannot continue as an American war fighter. I just won't, Dad. It just sickens me day in and day out, and it is treason against my King, against my real Kingdom and home. . . . I am no longer a child, and will not continue to act as if I am. . . . I am not running from what is hard, Dad, but rather strapping myself to a new cross.[11]

The moment of truth came one day when it was Joshua's job to interrogate a young Saudi Arabian man, a twenty-two-year-old, self-declared jihadi who readily admitted that he had come to Iraq to fight against foreign invaders of a Muslim country. "Finally," said Joshua, "I'll not just be dancing interrogatives with taxi drivers. I'm actually going to be talking to the real deal."[12]

But Joshua found himself unnerved by the young jihadi's confidence and self-possession during the interrogation. After trying, unsuccessfully, to put him off balance by some rapid-fire, aggressive questions, he asked the young man a simple question: "Why did you come here to Iraq to kill?" Now it was Joshua's turn to be off balance, as the jihadi immediately fired back at him, "Why did *you* come here to kill?" Joshua denied that his purpose was to kill anyone, explaining (rather hollowly) that he had come "to do his job, to defend the Iraqi people . . . I have a duty to my country, and I'm fulfilling that duty." The jihadi paused, then observed: "You are a strange man. If the United States didn't want people to be killed, they would have sent someone else, not soldiers."

Then the jihadi really struck a nerve, confronting Joshua about the contradictions between his professed Christianity and his participation in an unjust war: "You call yourself a Christian, but you don't act like the one you call Christ, and you don't follow his teachings—to love your enemies, to turn the other cheek." Joshua was speechless, thinking to himself, "Now *this* is an ironic moment, Joshua. Here you are sitting across the table from a declared jihadist, and here he is giving *you* a lesson on the Sermon on the Mount." After a pregnant silence, Joshua spoke: "I think, actually, you're *right*. There's something *wrong* here."

Joshua ended the interrogation. He went to his commanding officer and told him:

> "I can't interrogate this guy anymore, because if I go back in there I'll just see him as a person. I don't *care* to exploit him of his information. I want to talk to him man to man, about the things that matter—to him and to me. I want to talk to him about Islam, Christianity, Jesus, the cycle of vengeance. I'm just going to see a twenty-two-year-old Saudi Arabian

kid looking for answers, just like I'm a twenty-four-year-old American kid looking for answers. If you want to exploit him for intelligence, you're going to have to find someone else to do it, because I've lost my objectivity."

Soon after, Joshua began the formal process of applying for conscientious objector status. To his surprise, his commanding officer was supportive of his decision. "He respected me, applauded me for following my conscience, for taking the hard way, not the easy way. And that was pretty universal. People didn't necessarily agree with me, but they felt I was honorably going about trying to resolve my conflict with my conscience." He returned to the United States in January 2005 and was honorably discharged from the Army a few months later.

After his return to the United States, Joshua enrolled in the playwriting and nonfiction writing program. He wrote two plays about his experiences in Iraq, "Returns" and "The Interrogation Room." He received regular invitations to speak at gatherings of anti-war organizations like Iraq Veterans Against the War, Catholic Peace Fellowship, and Pax Christi. He was featured in the documentaries "Soldiers of Conscience" and "Iraq for Sale." At one point he began taking courses at the University of Chicago Divinity School. For a time he considered the possibility of becoming a Jesuit priest, after the example of other former soldiers like Francis of Assisi and Ignatius Loyola.

Sadly, Joshua was diagnosed with Stage IV lung cancer in November 2011. He believed the likely cause of the cancer had been inhalation of toxic fumes from the burn pits for refuse at Abu Ghraib prison. He died nine months later, at age thirty-two, while undergoing treatment in New York City. During his journey with cancer supportive family and friends created a website for him, on which a video titled "A Word of Thanks" was posted as a way for Joshua to express his gratitude for the love and support he had received during his illness. "I prefer the person I am right now," he says, with a voice obviously weakened by illness, "to the person that I was before I was diagnosed with cancer. I've really been *reborn*." Significantly, he added that his illness had given him a consoling feeling of solidarity with suffering people in Iraq: "One of the things that I have come to feel about my diagnosis . . . is a sense of relief that I get to share in the sufferings of the Iraqis."

Before I left Iowa City to drive back to Chicago, I asked Joshua to autograph my copy of *Letters from Abu Ghraib*. When I got home, I discovered that he had inscribed a verse from the King James Bible above his signature: "But be of good cheer; I have overcome the world!" (Jn 16:33).

AWAKENING FROM THE SLEEP
OF INHUMANITY

Claribel Alegria is a Nicaraguan poet who was haunted by the cruel oppression of her people during the Somoza dictatorship. In "Nocturnal Visits," she allows that it is only right that her sleep should be disturbed by the "shouting" of the people:

> At night I listen to their phantoms
> shouting in my ear
> shaking me out of lethargy
> issuing me commands
> I think of their tattered lives
> of their feverish hands
> reaching out to seize ours.
> It's not that they're begging
> they're demanding
> they've earned the right to order us
> to break up our sleep
> to come awake
> to shake off once and for all
> this lassitude.[13]

Encounters with the unjust suffering of others have the potential to unsettle us, shake us up, *wake* us up. An uneasy conscience can shock us out of our moral complacency, triggering a kind of holy confusion that has the potential, in turn, to bring about a change of heart. Jon Sobrino writes:

> The fundamental change . . . consists of an awakening, but from another type of sleep, or better, from a nightmare—the sleep of inhumanity. It is the awakening to the reality of an oppressed and subjugated world, a world whose liberation is the basic task of every human being, so that in this way human beings may finally come to be human.[14]

"I will give them a new heart and put a new spirit within them," says the prophet Ezekiel. "I will remove the stony heart from their bodies and replace it with a natural heart" (Ez 11:19, NAB). The "natural heart" of which he speaks is an open heart, a compassionate heart, a heart capable of being moved to compassion and indignation, and of moving *us* to an appropriately human response. The "stony heart" is characterized not so much by cruelty as by *apathy* or indifference—a kind of numbness or affective unresponsiveness to the pain of others. I am reminded of a talk I once attended by Sister Dianna Ortiz titled "Torture: Where Is the Outrage?" in which she lamented the seeming absence of appropriate shame and outrage in the response of the American public to the torture scandals of the Bush administration.

There is a conflict within all of us between what Reinhold Schneider called *"Agonie"* (agony) and *"Narkose"* (numbness).[15] For him, numbness was a metaphor for apathy or complacency, while "agony" was associated with compassion, the capacity to be inwardly moved by social suffering. Dorothee Soelle describes the tension like this:

> The conflict consists of the contradiction between the avoidance of suffering, not-having-seen and not-wanting-to-see

anything, and seeking to protect oneself with diverse and increasingly improving means of numbing, on the one hand; and
the preferential option for victims wherein [we] voluntarily
enter into the pain of others and, in the extreme case, choose
the pain of death, on the other.[16]

The agony of crucified people should be a wake-up call for all of
us. The torture of human beings *should* haunt us, bother us, madden
us, shame us, and hopefully, put the "fear of God" into us. We should
beware of getting too comfortable with injustice and cruelty. "Jesus
will be in agony until the end of the world," wrote Blaise Pascal, a
seventeenth-century philosopher and mathematician. "There must
be no sleeping during that time."[17]

RISING FROM THE DEAD

The literal idea of a miraculous, bodily resurrection after death is an
intellectual stumbling block for most people in the contemporary
world. But there are different ways to imagine what it means to die
and come back, to be reborn, to rise from the dead. Even so, the
kind of emotional and spiritual rebirth that some torture survivors
experience—a kind of rising from the dead while they are still
alive—is perhaps equally miraculous and improbable.

Those who do not survive are obviously never able to make it
back to the land of the living—either because they are tortured to
death or because the torturers kill them when they are no longer
considered useful. Others, because of the profound and disabling
nature of their trauma, are never quite able to return to some sem-
blance of ordinary life and human community. Still others—who
might otherwise have the potential to recover—end up stranded
in a hellish post-trauma world, forever reliving their torture, simply
because adequate resources for support and healing are unavailable
to them. I remember, with sadness, the stricken face of a young
Guatemalan man in an impoverished rural area of Totonicapan

who was so immobilized by fear that he had been unable to leave his home for years. Modern medicines for anxiety, depression, and post-traumatic stress could have done wonders for him, but they were out of the question because they were unavailable.

But some torture survivors *are* able to come back to life, to rise again. It may take a long time for people who have, for all intents and purposes, experienced a kind of emotional and spiritual death. I am thinking of Matilde de la Sierra, a physician who was tortured and raped because of her work with the Mayan people in the rural highlands of Guatemala. She writes:

> I walk without destination, as a dead woman walking, a mutilated entity. I try to smile and laugh, but deep down there is a sadness that won't go away. We survivors of torture try to pretend. I try to pretend that all is well now, that the past is past. But it really isn't past. It is with me each day.[18]

Matilde's recovery can be likened to a traumatic experience of dying and a long process of rebirth. For her, the healing process has involved learning to feel again, to experience some measure of trust again, to allow herself to love and be loved again. These are not easy things for someone who was violated so profoundly. Matilde was initially terrified of love, doubted it, resisted it. "I felt like a dirty woman, a piece of garbage, nothing," she explained. "What is love? Who can love a dirty woman? Love doesn't exist!"[19]

A crucial ingredient in Matilde's recovery has been her relationship with her husband, Jim, whom she met in the 1990s while living at the Su Casa shelter for Central American refugees and asylum seekers in Chicago. The poignant story of the delicate and halting unfolding of their relationship was featured in a National Public Radio series.[20] Beneath her fragile and timid external appearance, Jim sensed a mysterious hidden strength in Matilde, a capacity for perseverance in the face of suffering and adversity, a quiet dignity that remained in spite of all she had been through. *Beneath the*

Blindfold, a powerful 2012 documentary on survivors of torture that features Matilde and Jim, gives moving evidence of her gentle but indomitable spirit and also offers a glimpse of the love between them that has been so crucial in her recovery.[21]

Another ingredient in Matilde's recovery has been her participation in meaningful social action. For years, she has been a wounded healer. For her, this has taken the form of publicly telling her own story as a way to raise consciousness about the ongoing global scandal of torture and to work for its abolition. She was particularly grieved by Abu Ghraib and continues to be dismayed by the unjust incarceration and maltreatment of prisoners in the US prison at Guantanamo Bay. Matilde and Jim have also participated regularly in public vigils against torture, including one they organize in downtown Chicago on June 26 of every year, the day marked by the United Nations to honor survivors of torture. They sometimes have to endure verbal abuse from people who would rather not be reminded of torture.

Jim also takes a trip every November from Chicago to Fort Benning, Georgia, where he participates in the annual protest against the School of the Americas, the US military training program for Latin American military officers whose graduates have been responsible for some of the most shocking human rights violations and atrocities in Latin America over the last several decades. Each year Jim lends his beautiful voice for a somber ritual of mourning and remembrance, helping to sing a seemingly endless litany of the names of Latin American men, women, and children who have died by violence and torture. Hanging around Jim's neck is a large laminated photo of Matilde's father, Arnaldo, one of Guatemala's fifty thousand *desaparecidos*. The names, including Arnaldo's, are sung, and the people respond in song: "Presente!" *(Present! Here! He is present! She is here! They are here!)* The spirits of the tortured, the disappeared, and the dead are remembered, summoned, invoked. And, as they are felt and acknowledged in tears and loving remembrance, they come back to life.

A sacred spark of life at the core of the human person may appear to be extinguished by cruelty and injustice, but it can be rekindled through love. The beloved is not dead and gone forever, but is found to be alive and well. "Why do you look for the living among the dead?" (Lk 24:5). This is perhaps the mysterious secret at the heart of the story of the dying and rising of the tortured Christ. "Jesus believed above all—and for all—in a life before death," writes Dorothee Soelle. "The resurrection, this spark of life, was already in him. And only because of this God-in-him were they unable to kill him."[22]

Etty Hillesum, a soulful young Jewish woman from the Netherlands who perished at Auschwitz along with her family, wrote in her diary about something analogous to the spark of the divine within the human person (known as the *shekinah* in her Jewish tradition), referring to it as "that little piece of God in ourselves" that we must defend and try to keep alive, in ourselves and others, *no matter what*. This is a challenge for each of us and all of us, but the stakes are especially high for the souls of crucified people. Etty's words are a fitting conclusion to this book:

> It is all we can manage these days and also all that really matters: that we safeguard that little piece of You, God, in ourselves. And perhaps in others as well. Alas, there doesn't seem to be much You Yourself can do about our circumstances, about our lives. Neither do I hold You responsible.
>
> You cannot help us but we must help You and defend Your dwelling place inside us to the last.[23]

NOTES

PREFACE

1. Gustavo Gutiérrez, *On Job: God-Talk and the Suffering of the Innocent* (Maryknoll, NY: Orbis Books, 1987), xvii.

2. For a beautiful photographic tour of this amazing place, see Martin Biddle, Gideon Avni, Jon Seligman, and Tamar Winter, *The Church of the Holy Sepulchre* (New York: Rizzoli, 2000).

3. See, for example, Mircea Eliade, "The Symbol of the Center," in *Images and Symbols: Studies in Religious Symbolism* (Princeton, NJ: Princeton University Press, 1991). The center of the world is what C. G. Jung would call an archetypal symbol. See, for example, Jung's reflections on the center and mandala symbolism in *Man and His Symbols* and *Memories, Dreams, and Reflections*.

4. John G. Niehardt, *Black Elk Speaks: Being the Life Story of a Holy Man of the Oglala Sioux* (Lincoln: University of Nebraska Press, 1931), 43.

5. For a personal account of her creative process and links to images of all fourteen paintings, see Gwyneth Leech, "A New Journey: Stations of the Cross for Our Time," *Faith and Form* 39/1. Also see "Cross Connections: Christ's Passion Re-Imagined Through the Lens of Contemporary Torture, Terror, and Tragedy," *Counterpunch* (November 11–13, 2005), http://www.counterpunch .org/2005/11/11/cross-connections/. Also see the artist's website, http://www .gwynethleech.com/.

6. Leech, "A New Journey,"

7. Leech, "Cross Connections."

INTRODUCTION

1. Sometimes known as "The Quaker Hymn," the original words to "How Can I Keep from Singing?" were published in a hymnal by Robert Lowry in 1869. The author is unknown. The above verse was added by Doris Plenn

around 1950; she taught it to folk singer Pete Seeger, who popularized the song in the folk movement of the 1960s.

2. For a history of the Kovler Center by some of its founding and sustaining mothers and fathers, see Mary Fabri, Mario Gonzalez, Marianne Joyce, and Mary Black, "Caring for Torture Survivors: The Marjorie Kovler Center," in *The New Humanitarians: Inspiration, Innovations, and Blueprints for Visionaries,* ed. Chris E. Stout (Santa Barbara, CA: Praeger, 2008).

3. See Jon Sobrino, "Human Rights and Oppressed Peoples: Historical-Theological Reflections," in *Truth and Memory: The Church and Human Rights in El Salvador and Guatemala,* ed. M. A. Hayes and D. Tombs, 134–58 (London: Gracewing, 2001).

4. Jon Sobrino, *Where Is God? Earthquake, Terrorism, Barbarity, and Hope* (Maryknoll, NY: Orbis Books, 2004), 45.

5. John Neafsey, *A Sacred Voice Is Calling: Personal Vocation and Social Conscience* (Maryknoll, NY: Orbis Books, 2006).

6. This heart-grounded ethical metaphor comes from Irish theologian Enda McDonagh. See "The Structure and Basis of Moral Experience," in *Introduction to Christian Ethics: A Reader,* ed. Ronald P. Hamel, and Kenneth R. Himes, 106–19 (Mahwah, NJ: Paulist Press, 1989).

7. Jennifer Harbury, *Truth, Torture, and the American Way: The History and Consequences of US Involvement in Torture* (Boston: Beacon Press, 2005).

8. For an insightful history and analysis of the APA torture controversy, see Neil Altman, "Psychoanalysis in the Political World: The Case of the American Psychological Association and Torture," in *The Analyst in the Inner City: Race, Class, and Culture Through a Psychoanalytic Lens* (Florence, KY: Routledge, 2009). See also Stephen Soldz, "Psychologists, Torture, and Civil Society: Complicity, Institutional Failure, and the Struggle for Professional Transformation," in *The United States and Torture: Interrogation, Incarceration, and Abuse,* ed. Marjorie Cohn, 177–202 (New York: NYU Press, 2012).

9. Louis J. Puhl, SJ, *The Spiritual Exercises of Saint Ignatius* (Chicago: Loyola Press, 1951), 28.

10. Ignacio Ellacuría, quoted in Jon Sobrino, *Jesus the Liberator: A Historical-Theological Reading of Jesus of Nazareth* (Maryknoll, NY: Orbis Books, 1993), 262–63. Original in Ignacio Ellacuría, "Las Iglesias latinoamericanas interpelan a la Iglesia de Espanaa," *Sal Terrae* 826 (1982): 230.

11. William Lynch, S.J. has done some wonderful writing on imagination; see especially *Images of Hope: Imagination as Healer of the Hopeless* (Notre Dame,

IN: University of Notre Dame Press, 1965). Also see Paul Crowley's summary of Lynch's work on "The Christic Imagination," in *Unwanted Wisdom: Suffering, the Cross, and Hope,* 46–51 (New York: Continuum, 2005).

1. TORTURE AND THE CROSS

1. Elizabeth Johnson, *Quest for the Living God: Mapping Frontiers in the Theology of God* (New York: Continuum, 2007), 65.

2. Countee Cullen, "The Black Christ," in *My Soul's High Song: The Collected Writings of Countee Cullen,* ed. Gerald Early (New York: Anchor Books, 1991), 207.

3. Gerard Manley Hopkins, "As Kingfishers Catch Fire," in *Gerard Manley Hopkins: Poems and Prose,* ed. Catherine Phillips (Penguin Classics, 1985).

4. See, for example, John P. Meier, *A Marginal Jew: Rethinking the Historical Jesus* (New York: Doubleday, 1991). See also Gerard S. Sloyan, *The Crucifixion of Jesus: History, Myth, Faith* (Minneapolis: Fortress Press, 1995); and John Dominic Crossan, *The Historical Jesus: The Life of a Mediterranean Jewish Peasant* (San Francisco: HarperSanFrancisco, 1991).

5. See Meier, *A Marginal Jew,* 168–71.

6. Tacitus, *The Annals and the Histories* (New York: Modern Library/Random House, 2003), Book 15, chap. 44, 327.

7. Flavius Josephus, *Jewish Antiquities,* 18:63, quoted in Crossan, *The Historical Jesus,* 373. This version of the passage, with interpolation by Christian scribes deleted, is regarded by scholars as likely to be most true to the original words of Josephus.

8. See Dorothee Soelle and Luise Schottroff, *Jesus of Nazareth* (Louisville, KY: Westminster John Knox Press, 2000), 113–24.

9. See "That Charming Pontius Pilate," in John Dominic Crossan, *Jesus: A Revolutionary Biography* (San Francisco: HarperOne, 2009), 136–40.

10. Philo, *Embassy to Gaius,* 301, quoted in Daniel Harrington, SJ, *Jesus: A Historical Portrait* (Cincinnati: St. Anthony Messenger Press, 2007), 70.

11. See Albert Nolan, *Jesus Before Christianity* (Maryknoll, NY: Orbis Books, 1992), 155.

12. Paula Fredriksen, *From Jesus to Christ: The Origins of the New Testament Images of Jesus,* 2nd ed. (New Haven, CT: Yale University Press, 2000 [1988]), 120.

13. Susan Neiman, *Evil in Modern Thought: An Alternative History of Philosophy,* (Princeton, NJ: Princeton University Press, 2002), 256.

14. Martin Hengel, *Crucifixion in the Ancient World and the Folly of the Message of the Cross* (Philadelphia: Fortress Press, 1977), 22.

15. Ibid., 86–87.

16. Josephus, *Jewish War* 5:447–51, quoted in Crossan, *The Historical Jesus,* 126.

17. Dorothee Soelle, *Theology for Skeptics: Reflections on God* (Minneapolis: Fortress Press, 1995), 102.

18. Ignacio Ellacuría, "The Crucified People," in *Systematic Theology: Perspectives from Liberation Theology,* ed. Jon Sobrino and Ignacio Ellacuría (Maryknoll, NY: Orbis Books, 1993), 264.

19. See Teresa Whitfield, *Paying the Price: Ignacio Ellacuría and the Murdered Jesuits of El Salvador* (Philadelphia: Temple University Press, 1995).

20. Archbishop Oscar Romero, *The Violence of Love,* comp. and ed. James R. Brockman (Maryknoll, NY: Orbis Books, 2004), 191–92.

21. Jon Sobrino, "Jesus' Approach as a Paradigm for Mission," in *Jesus of Galilee: Contextual Christology for the Twenty-First Century,* ed. Robert Lassalle-Klein (Maryknoll, NY: Orbis Books, 2011), 87.

22. Ibid., 88.

23. Johann Baptist Metz, "Communicating a Dangerous Memory," in *Love's Strategy: The Political Theology of Johann Baptist Metz,* ed. J. K. Downey (Harrisburg, PA: Trinity Press International, 1999), 144.

24. This phrase is from Frederick Buechner, *The Hungering Dark* (San Francisco: Harper and Row, 1985), 29.

25. This jarring phrase from Paolo Ricca is quoted in John Hoffmeyer, "Torture and Theology of the Cross," *Dialog* 47/3 (2008): 245. Ricca is a theologian active in Christian Action for the Abolition of Torture (ACAT), the movement against torture in Europe.

26. Ricca, in ibid., 245.

27. Eduardo Galeano, "A Profession of Faith," in *The Book of Embraces* (New York: W. W. Norton, 1989), 245.

28. See Neil Elliot, "Seeing the Crucified in the Real World," *The Witness* (March 2, 2005), available at http://www.thewitness.org/article.php?id=734.

29. See Melanie Thernstrom, "The Crucifixion of Matthew Shepard," *Vanity Fair* (March 1999).

30. "Three Whites Indicted in Dragging Death of Black Man in Texas." CNN.com, July 6, 1998, available at http://edition.cnn.com/US/9807/06/dragging.death.02/.

31. The Matthew Shepard and James Bird Jr. Hate Crimes Prevention Act was passed by the US Congress on October 22, 2009, and signed into law by President Obama on October 29, 2009.

32. See James Allen, *Without Sanctuary: Lynching Photography in America* (Santa Fe, NM: Twin Palms Publishers, 2000).

33. James Cone, *The Cross and the Lynching Tree* (Maryknoll, NY: Orbis Books, 2011).

34. These lines are from the poem "Christ Recrucified," written by Countee Cullen when he was nineteen years old. The poem was published only once, in the October 1922 issue of *Kelley's Magazine*. It has never been published since in any collection of Cullen's works but appears to have evolved into a later poem, "The Black Christ." See Gerald Early, ed., *My Soul's High Song: The Collected Works of Countee Cullen* (New York: Doubleday, 1991), 207–36.

35. Some of this material is adapted from my book *A Sacred Voice Is Calling: Personal Vocation and Social Conscience* (Maryknoll, NY: Orbis Books, 2006).

36. Reinhold Schneider, *Winter in Wein* (1903–58), quoted in Dorothee Soelle, *The Silent Cry: Mysticism and Resistance* (Minneapolis: Augsburg Fortress, 2001), 154.

37. Dietrich Bonhoeffer, *Letters and Papers from Prison* (New York: MacMillan, 1953), 188.

38. Elizabeth Johnson, *She Who Is: The Mystery of God in Feminist Theological Discourse* (New York: Crossroad, 1992), 264.

39. Elie Wiesel, *Night* (New York: Avon Books, 1969), 75–76.

40. Elizabeth Johnson, *Quest for the Living God: Mapping Frontiers in the Theology of God* (New York: Continuum, 2007), 57.

41. Dorothee Soelle, *Suffering* (Philadelphia: Fortress Press, 1975), 148.

42. Jon Sobrino, *The Principle of Mercy* (Maryknoll, NY: Orbis Books, 1994), 8.

43. For authoritative reviews of the carnage of the Guatemalan war, see *Guatemala Never Again! The Official Report of the Human Rights Office, Archdiocese of Guatemala* (Maryknoll, NY: Orbis Books, 1999). Also see Daniel Rothenberg, ed., *Memory of Silence: The Guatemalan Truth Commission Report* (New York: Palgrave Macmillan, 2012).

2. THE SCANDAL OF TORTURE

1. Kurt Vonnegut, *Cat's Cradle* (New York: Dial Press, 2010 [1963]), 68.

2. Oscar Avila, "Torture Survivors Relive the Horrors," *Chicago Tribune*, May 14, 2004.

3. Ibid.

4. Elaine Scarry, *The Body in Pain: The Making and Unmaking of a World* (New York: Oxford University Press, 1985), 28.

5. See John Perry, *Torture: Religious Ethics and National Security* (Maryknoll, NY: Orbis Books, 2005), 32.

6. Frantz Fanon, *The Wretched of the Earth* (New York: Grove Press, 1968), 281.

7. Quotation from Khalid Sheik Mohammed, International Committee of the Red Cross, "ICRC Report on the Treatment of Fourteen 'High Value Detainees' in CIA Custody" (February 2007), International Committee of the Red Cross, 37, available at http://assets.nybooks.com/media/doc/2010/04/22/icrc-report.pdf.

8. Peter Finn, "Detainee Who Gave False Iraq Data Dies in Prison in Libya," *Washington Post,* May 12, 2009.

9. Ibid.

10. Amnesty International, *Political Prisoners in South Vietnam* (London: Amnesty International Publications, n.d.), quoted in Scarry, *The Body in Pain,* 41–42.

11. Dianna Ortiz (with Patricia Davis), *The Blindfold's Eyes: My Journey from Torture to Truth* (Maryknoll, NY: Orbis Books, 2002), 37.

12. Tim Golden, "In US Report, Brutal Details of Two Afghan Inmates' Deaths," *New York Times,* May 20, 2005.

13. Ibid.

14. Dilawar's story is featured in the Academy Award nominated 2007 documentary "Taxi to the Dark Side," directed by Alex Gibney.

15. Ibid.

16. Golden, "In US Report, Brutal Details of Two Afghan Inmates' Deaths." Also see Steven Miles, *Oath Betrayed: Torture, Medical Complicity, and the War on Terror* (New York: Random House, 2006), 69.

17. Interviews with Lawrence Wilkerson, in "Taxi to the Dark Side."

18. Wilkerson interview, "The Court-Martial of Willie Brand," *60 Minutes* (March 2006).

19. According to a December 2012 poll, only 25 percent of Americans said that torture of suspected terrorists who may know details about future attacks is *never* justified, 19 percent said it was *always* justified, 28 percent said it was

sometimes justified, and 16 percent said it is *rarely* justified. See "Torture Poll: Most Americans See Torture as Justified at Times," *Huffington Post,* December 14, 2012, available at http://www.huffingtonpost.com/2012/12/14/torture-poll-2012_n_2301492.html.

20. Graham Greene, *Reflections,* quoted in Daniel Berrigan, *The Kings and Their Gods: The Pathology of Power* (Grand Rapids, MI: Eerdmans, 2008), 32.

21. Email, August 2, 2004, from [REDACTED] to [REDACTED], quoted in Mark Danner, "We Are All Torturers Now," *New York Times,* January 6, 2005; also in idem, *Stripping Bare the Body: Politics, Violence, War* (New York: Nation Books, 2009), 417.

22. See, for example, Andy Worthington, *The Guantanamo Files: The Stories of the 774 Detainees in America's Illegal Prison,* (London: Pluto Press, 2007); Lawrence Wilkerson, "Some Truths About Guantanamo Bay," *Washington Note,* March 17, 2009, available at http://www.thewashingtonnote.com/archives/2009/03/some_truths_abo/?ref=fp2.

23. Remarks of President George W. Bush, East Room of the White House, September 6, 2006.

24. Quoted in Jane Mayer, *The Dark Side: The Inside Story of How the War on Terror Turned into a War on American Ideals* (New York: Doubleday, 2008), 9–10.

25. See Jane Mayer, "Outsourcing Torture: The Secret History of America's 'Extraordinary Rendition' Program," in *The United States and Torture: Interrogation Incarceration, Abuse,* ed. Marjorie Cohn, 137–60 (New York: New York University Press, 2011).

26. "ICRC Report," 81.

27. Ibid., 8–9.

28. Scott Shane, "Waterboarding Used 266 Times on Two Suspects," *New York Times,* April 20, 2009. According to a 2005 Justice Department memo, the CIA revealed not only the 266 incidents of waterboarding but that it had destroyed videotapes that had been made of Zubayda's interrogation and torture.

29. "ICRC Report," 34.

30. Peter Finn and Anne Komblut, "Obama Creates Indefinite Detention System for Prisoners at Guantanamo Bay," *Washington Post,* March 11, 2011.

31. Jane Mayer, "Torture and Obama's Drone Program." *New Yorker,* February 15, 2012.

32. Charlie Savage, "Despair Drives Guantanamo Detainees to Revolt," *New York Times,* April 25, 2013.

33. George J. Annas, Sondra S. Crosby, and Leonard H. Glantz, "Guantanamo Bay: A Medical Ethics–Free Zone?" *New England Journal of Medicine* (June 12, 2013).

34. Laura Poitras, "Death of a Prisoner," *New York Times,* January 10, 2013.

35. Associated Press, "Guantanamo Death Was Suicide, US Finds," *Salon* (San Juan, Puerto Rico), November 29, 2012.

36. John Conroy, *Unspeakable Acts, Ordinary People: The Dynamics of Torture* (Berkeley and Los Angeles: University of California Press, 2000).

37. Primo Levi, *The Reawakening* (New York: Touchstone, 1965), 228.

38. Neil Altman, *The Analyst in the Inner City: Race, Class, and Culture Through a Psychoanalytic Lens* (New York: Routledge, 2010), 295.

39. Stanley Milgram, "The Perils of Obedience," *Harper's Magazine* (December 1973), 62–77. Also see idem, *Obedience to Authority: An Experimental View* (New York: Harper and Row, 1974).

40. Joshua E. S. Phillips, *None of Us Were Like This Before: American Soldiers and Torture* (New York: Verso, 2010), 40.

41. Interview with Pfc. Damien Corsetti, in "Taxi to the Dark Side."

42. Robert Jay Lifton, "Conditions of Atrocity," in *Crimes of War: Iraq,* ed. R. Falk, I. Gendzier, and R. J. Lifton (New York: Nation Books, 2006), 340.

43. Zimbardo, "Power Turns Good Soldiers into Bad Apples," *Boston Globe,* May 9, 2004.

44. Philip Zimbardo, *The Lucifer Effect: Understanding How Good People Turn Evil* (New York: Random House, 2008). Lucifer imagery and mythology originated in verses from Isaiah that were originally about the humiliating comeuppance of an insolent, arrogant king in ancient Babylon: "How you are fallen from heaven, O Lucifer, Son of the Morning!" (Is 14:12, KJB).

45. Lifton, "Conditions of Atrocity," 340.

46. Ibid., 340–41.

47. For example, see the six-hundred page report of the Constitution Project's Task Force on Detainee Treatment, released in April 2013, available at http://www.nytimes.com/interactive/2013/04/16/world/16torture-report.html?ref=world.

48. Noam Chomsky, "The Torture Memos," in *Hopes and Prospects* (Chicago: Haymarket Books, 2010), 268.

49. Mayer, *The Dark Side,* 175.

50. Aleksandr Solzhenitsyn, *The Gulag Archipelago, 1918–1956* (New York: HarperCollins, 2002 [1985]), 311.

51. See Rita Nakashima Brock and Gabriella Lettini, *Soul Repair: Recovering from Moral Injury after War* (Boston: Beacon Press, 2012).

52. William Sloane Coffin, *Passion for the Possible* (Louisville, KY: Westminster/John Knox Press, 2004), 50.

3. CRUCIFIED PEOPLES

1. Elizabeth Johnson, *Quest for the Living God: Mapping Frontiers in the Theology of God* (New York: Continuum, 2007), 78.

2. Eduardo Galeano, "The Nobodies," *Open Veins of Latin America: Five Centuries of the Pillage of a Continent* (New York: Monthly Review Press, 1973; originally published in Spanish in 1971), quoted in Paul Farmer, *Pathologies of Power: Health, Human Rights, and the New War on the Poor* (Berkeley and Los Angeles: University of California Press, 2005), 1.

3. See Ignacio Ellacuría, "The Crucified People," in *Systematic Theology: Perspectives from Liberation Theology,* ed. Jon Sobrino and Ignacio Ellacuría (Maryknoll, NY: Orbis Books, 1993), 266.

4. Frantz Fanon, *The Wretched of the Earth* (New York: Grove Press, 1968).

5. See Teresa Whitfield, *Paying the Price: Ignacio Ellacuría and the Murdered Jesuits of El Salvador* (Philadelphia: Temple University Press, 1995).

6. For an English translation of some of Martín-Baro's writings, see *Writings for a Liberation Psychology,* ed. Adrianne Aron and Shawn Corn (Cambridge, MA: Harvard University Press, 1996).

7. Jon Sobrino, *The Principle of Mercy: Taking the Crucified People from the Cross* (Maryknoll, NY: Orbis Books, 1994), 50–51.

8. The World Bank estimates that 1.3 billion people (about 20 percent of the world's population) live in extreme poverty (defined as less than US$1.25 a day), 2.5 billion people (over one-third of the world) live on less than US$2.00 a day, and 5 billion people (70 percent) live on less than US$10.00 a day. See http://www.worldbank.org/en/topic/poverty/overview.

9. Leonardo and Clodovis Boff, *Introducing Liberation Theology* (Maryknoll, NY: Orbis Books, 2004), 31.

10. Sobrino, *The Principle of Mercy,* 256.

11. Ellacuría, "The Crucified People," 267.

12. Robert M. Poole, "What Became of the Taino?" *Smithsonian* (October 2011), available at http://www.smithsonianmag.com/people-places/What-Became-of-the-Taino.html?c=y&page=1.

13. In Gustavo Gutiérrez, *Las Casas: In Search of the Poor of Jesus Christ* (Maryknoll, NY: Orbis Books, 1993), 29.

14. For an excellent short biography of Bartolomé de Las Casas, see Robert Ellsberg, "God or Gold: Bartolomé de Las Casas," in *Not Less than Everything: Catholic Writers on Heroes of Conscience from Oscar Romero to Joan of Arc*, ed. Catherine Wolff, 116–25 (New York: HarperCollins, 2013).

15. Bartolomé de Las Casas, *A Brief Account of the Destruction of the Indies* (Thousand Oaks, CA: BN Publishing, 2009).

16. Bartolomé de Las Casas, from *História de las Indias*, quoted in Gustavo Gutiérrez, *Las Casas* (Maryknoll, NY: Orbis Books, 1993), 62.

17. See Paul Farmer, "A History of the Present Illness," in *Haiti: After the Earthquake* (New York: Public Affairs, 2011), 121–39.

18. Robert Debs Heinl and Nancy Gordon Heinl, *Written in Blood: The Story of the Haitian People, 1492–1995* (New York: University Press of America, 1996), 25–26.

19. Galeano, *Open Veins of Latin America*, 2.

20. John G. Neihardt, *Black Elk Speaks: Being the Life Story of a Holy Man of the Oglala Sioux* (Lincoln: University of Nebraska Press, 1932), 9.

21. See Edmund Hochschild, *King Leopold's Ghost: A Story of Greed, Terror, and Heroism in Colonial Africa* (New York: Mariner Books, 1999).

22. Ibid., 161.

23. Ibid., 161–62.

24. Ibid., 121.

25. Ibid., 225–34.

26. Ibid.

27. Joseph Conrad, *Heart of Darkness* (Mineola, NY: Dover Publications, 1990 [1902]), 3–4.

28. Johnson, *Quest for the Living God*, 80.

29. See Jeffrey Gettleman, "The World's Worst War," *New York Times*, December 15, 2012. Also see Jason K. Stearns, *Dancing in the Glory of Monsters: The Collapse of the Congo and the Great War of Africa* (New York: PublicAffairs, 2011).

30. See Robin Wright, "Your Cell Phone, Congo's Misery," *CNN: Inside Africa*, November 28, 2011. Also see John Prendergast, "Can You Hear Congo Now? Cell Phones, Conflict Minerals, and the Worst Sexual Violence in the World," April 1, 2009, available at http://www.enoughproject.org.

31. Paul Farmer, "How We Can Save Millions of Lives," *Washington Post*, November 17, 2011. For an excellent biography of Farmer, see Tracy Kidder,

Mountains Beyond Mountains: The Quest of Dr. Paul Farmer, A Man Who Would Cure the World (New York: Random House, 2004).

32. Farmer, *Pathologies of Power*, 144.

33. Ibid., xi–xii.

34. William Sloane Coffin, *Passion for the Possible* (Louisville, KY: Westminster/John Knox Press, 2004), 50.

35. Ibid., 176.

36. Julfikar Ali Manik et al., "Western Firms Feel Pressure as Toll Rises in Bangladesh," *New York Times,* April 25, 2013. The final death toll was 1,129. Over four thousand poeple were injured. See also Sarah Stillman, "Death Traps: The Bangladesh Garment Factory Disaster," *New Yorker*, May 1, 2013.

37. Farmer, *Pathologies of Power*, 176.

38. For a running counter that tracks expenditures for the wars in both Iraq and Afghanistan, see http://costofwar.com.

39. Joseph Stiglitz and Linda Bilmes, *The Three Trillion Dollar War: The True Cost of the War in Iraq* (New York: W. W. Norton, 2008).

40. See http://www.iraqbodycount.org.

41. G. Burnham, R. Lafta, S. Doocy, and L. Roberts, "Mortality After the 2003 Invasion of Iraq: A Cross-sectional Cluster Sample Survey," *Lancet* (October 11, 2006); 368, 1421–28.

42. Excerpted from Claribel Alegria, "From the Bridge," in *Poetry Like Bread: Poets of the Political Imagination,* ed. Martin Espada (Willimantie, CT: Curbstone Press, 1994), 33.

43. Excerpted from James Russell Lowell, "The Present Crisis," *Yale Book of American Verse* (New Haven, CT: Yale University Press, 1912), 278.

4. THE WOUNDS OF TORTURE

1. Jacobo Timmerman, *Prisoner Without a Name, Cell Without a Number* (New York: Knopf, 1981), 32.

2. Jean Amery, *At the Mind's Limits: Contemplations of a Survivor of Auschwitz and Its Realities* (Bloomington: Indiana University Press, 1980), 34.

3. From a beautiful bluegrass hymn titled "By the Mark," written by Gillian Welch and David Rawlings, on Gillian Welch, *Revival,* album (Nashville, TN: Acony Records, 1996).

4. Judith Herman, *Trauma and Recovery* (New York: Basic Books, 1992), 53.

5. Desmond Tutu, *God Has a Dream* (New York: Doubleday, 2004), 40.

6. Marilyn McCord Adams, *Horrendous Evils and the Goodness of God,* Cornell Studies in the Philosophy of Religion (Ithaca, NY: Cornell University Press, 1999), 26–27.

7. Herman, *Trauma and Recovery,* 51.

8. Amery, *At the Mind's Limits,* 34.

9. Herman, *Trauma and Recovery,* 33.

10. *Diagnostic and Statistical Manual of Mental Disorders,* 5th ed. (Arlington, VA: American Psychiatric Association, 2013).

11. Guatemalan Commission for Historical Clarification, *Memory of Silence: The Guatemalan Truth Commission Report,* ed. Daniel Rothenberg (New York: Palgrave Macmillan, 2012), 156.

12. Robert Jay Lifton, *The Broken Connection* (Arlington, VA: American Psychiatric Publications, 1996), 171.

13. Guatemalan Commission for Historical Clarification, *Memory of Silence,* 146.

14. See, for example, the work of Dr. Maria Yellow Horse Brave Heart on historical trauma and grief among the Lakota people, discussed in "To Die and Come Back," chap. 6 of this book.

15. William Gorman, "Refugee Survivors of Torture: Trauma and Treatment," *Professional Psychology: Research and Practice* 32/5 (2001): 443–51.

16. William T. Cavanaugh, "Torture and Eucharist: A Regretful Update," in *Torture Is a Moral Issue: Christians, Jews, Muslims and People of Conscience Speak Out,* ed. G. Hunsinger (Grand Rapids, MI: Eerdmans, 2008), 96. See also idem, *Torture and Eucharist: Theology, Politics, and the Body of Christ* (Malden, MA: Blackwell Publishing, 1998).

5. CARING FOR TORTURE SURVIVORS

1. Izet Sarajlic, "Softy with a Touch of Sadness," trans. Charles Simic, in *Scar on the Stone: Contemporary Poetry from Bosnia,* ed. Chris Agee (Highgreen, England: Bloodaxe Books, 1998), 70.

2. Dr. Irene Martinez, quoted in Mary Fabri, Mario Gonzalez, Marianne Joyce, and Mary Black, "Caring for Torture Survivors: The Marjorie Kovler Center," in *The New Humanitarians: Inspiration, Innovations, and Blueprints for Visionaries,* ed. Chris E. Stout (Santa Barbara, CA: Praeger, 2008).

3. Establishing safety, according to Dr. Judith Herman, is the primary need of survivors of trauma and is a necessary precondition for the healing and

recovery process. Herman's work is discussed in the "Trauma and Recovery" section of this chapter.

4. "The Shamrock Shore." A beautiful version of this traditional Irish ballad is sung by Paul Brady on *Matt Molloy, Paul Brady, Tommy Peoples*, album (Danbury, CT: Green Linnet Records, 1993).

5. United Nations Convention Relating to the Status of Refugees (1951).

6. See Carol Bohmer and Amy Schuman, *Rejecting Refugees: Political Asylum in the Twenty-First Century* (New York: Routledge, 2008).

7. David Hollenbach, "Introduction," in *Driven from Home: Protecting the Rights of Forced Migrants,* Ed. David Hollenbach (Washington DC: Georgetown University Press, 2010), 2.

8. For an inspiring history of the US sanctuary movement, see Renny Golden and Michael McConnell, *Sanctuary, The New Underground Railroad* (Maryknoll, NY: Orbis Books, 1986).

9. Flynn McRoberts, "Group Provides Haven for Torture Survivors," *Chicago Tribune*, February 27, 1995. Sister Pat and Sister JoAnn are featured in the excellent 2013 documentary "Band of Sisters," produced and directed by Mary Fishman, http://www.bandofsistersmovie.com.

10. Judith Herman, *Trauma and Recovery* (New York: Basic Books, 1992), 3.

11. Leston Havens, *Coming to Life: Reflections on the Art of Psychotherapy* (Cambridge, MA: Harvard University Press, 1994), 1.

12. Herman, *Trauma and Recovery,* 176.

13. Pumla Gobodo-Madikizela, "Memory and Trauma," in *Truth and Lies: Stories from the Truth and Reconciliation Commission in South Africa*, ed. Jillian Edelstein (New York: Free Press, 2001), 27.

14. Herman, *Trauma and Recovery,* 188.

15. Ibid., 49.

16. Harry Guntrip, *Schizoid Phenomena, Object Relations, and the Self* (London: Karnac Books, 1968), 12.

17. Leonard Shengold uses the image of the Via Dolorosa in *Soul Murder: The Effects of Childhood Abuse and Deprivation* (New Haven, CT: Yale University Press, 1989), 290.

18. Herman, *Trauma and Recovery,* 207.

19. Dianna Ortiz (with Patricia Davis), *The Blindfold's Eyes: My Journey from Torture to Truth* (Maryknoll, NY: Orbis Books, 2002).

20. Neil Altman, "Experiences in a Public Clinic," in *The Analyst in the Inner City: Race, Class, and Culture Through a Psychoanalytic Lens* (Florence, KY: Routledge, 2009).

21. Nancy Scheper-Hughes, "A Talent for Life: Reflections on Human Vulnerability and Resilience," *Ethnos: Journal of Anthropology* 73/1 (March 2008): 25, 42.

22. Pilar Hernandez, David Gangsei, and David Engstrom, "Vicarious Resilience: A New Concept in Work with Those Who Survive Trauma," *Family Process* 46/2 (June 2007): 230.

6. HEALING OF NATIONS

1. Pumla Gobodo-Madikizela, "Memory and Trauma," in *Truth and Lies: Stories from the Truth and Reconciliation Commission in South Africa*, ed. Jillian Edelstein (New York: Free Press, 2001), 30.

2. Judith Herman, *Trauma and Recovery* (New York: Basic Books, 1992), 1.

3. Maria Yellow Horse Brave Heart, "From Intergenerational Trauma to Intergenerational Healing," talk, Fifth Annual White Bison Wellbriety Conference, Denver Colorado, April 22, 2005, in *Wellbriety* 6/6 (May 25, 2005), available at http://www.whitebison.org/magazine/2005/volume6/no6.htm.

4. Joseph Brings Plenty, "Save Wounded Knee," *New York Times*, April 11, 2013.

5. John G. Neihardt, *Black Elk Speaks: Being the Life Story of a Holy Man of the Oglala Sioux* (Lincoln: University of Nebraska Press, 1932), 270.

6. Maria Yellow Horse Brave Heart, "*Wakiksuyapi:* Carrying the Historical Trauma of the Lakota," available at http://discoveringourstory.wisdomoftheelders.org/ht_and_grief/Wakiksuyapi-HT.pdf.

7. Ibid.

8. Robert Jay Lifton, *Death in Life: Survivors of Hiroshima* (Chapel Hill: University of North Carolina Press, 1991), 201.

9. Robert Jay Lifton, *Witness to an Extreme Century: A Memoir* (New York: Free Press, 2011), 127–28.

10. Primo Levi, *If This Is a Man* and *The Truce* (London: Abacus, 1987), 96.

11. Dorothee Soelle, *Suffering* (Philadelphia: Fortress Press, 1975), 145–46.

12. From Elie Wiesel, *And the World Remained Silent* (1956), originally written in Yiddish and later edited into his book *Night* (1960), which did

not include this line. See Ruth Franklin's essay in *Elie Wiesel's Night (Bloom's Guides)*, ed. Harold Bloom (New York: Chelsea House Publications, 2008), 112.

13. Neihardt, *Black Elk Speaks*, 272–74.

14. REMHI, *Guatemala Never Again! The Official Report of the Human Rights Office, Archdiocese of Guatemala* (Maryknoll, NY: Orbis Books, 1999), xxiii. This is an abbreviated English-language version of the original Spanish report (1998).

15. See Daniel Rothenberg, ed., *Memory of Silence: The Guatemalan Truth Commission Report* (New York: Palgrave Macmillan, 2012), xxx. The worst periods of violence were during the regimes of General Romeo Lucas Garcia (1978–82), who was succeeded after a military coup by General Efrain Rios Montt (1982–83), who was succeeded after a military coup by General Oscar Mejia Victores (1983–86).

16. See Daniel Rothenberg, "Introduction," in ibid., xix–xli.

17. Francisco Goldman, *The Art of Political Murder: Who Killed the Bishop?* (New York: Grove Press, 2007), 23.

18. Juan José Gerardi Canedera, quoted in ibid., 12.

19. REMHI, *Guatemala Never Again*, xxv.

20. Goldman, *The Art of Political Murder*. See also Carolyn Curiel, "Murder in Guatemala," *New York Review of Books*, September 30, 2007. For more information on Francisco Goldman, see his website, http://www.francisco-goldman.com.

21. Rothenberg, *Memory of Silence*, 145–46.

22. Goldman, *The Art of Political Murder*, 239.

23. Sonia Perez-Diaz, "Efrain Rios Montt Trial: Former Soldier Implicates President Otto Pérez Molina in Civil War Atrocities," *Huffington Post*, April 4, 2013.

24. Elizabeth Johnson, *Quest for the Living God: Mapping Frontiers in the Theology of God* (New York: Continuum, 2007), 66.

25. Desmond Mpilo Tutu, *No Future Without Forgiveness* (New York: Doubleday, 1999).

26. Ismail Mahomed, quoted in ibid., 25.

27. Tutu, *No Future Without Forgiveness*, 143–44.

28. Ibid., 148. The original version of "Senzenina" is in the Xhosa/Zulu language; it became a popular anti-apartheid folk song, often sung at funerals and demonstrations.

29. Ibid., 150–51.

30. Ibid., 151.

31. Antjie Krog, a South African poet and journalist, covered the TRC hearings. See Antjie Krog, *The Country of My Skull: Guilt, Sorrow, and the Limits of Forgiveness* (New York: Broadway Books, 2000).

32. Pumla Gobodo-Madikizela, *A Human Being Died That Night: A South African Woman Confronts the Legacy of Apartheid* (New York: Houghton Mifflin, 2003).

33. Ibid., 119–20.

34. Michael Lapsley (with Stephen Karakashian), *Redeeming the Past: My Journey from Freedom Fighter to Healer* (Maryknoll, NY: Orbis Books, 2012).

7. GLIMPSES OF REDEMPTION

1. Julia Esquivel, "They Have Threatened Us with Resurrection," in *Threatened with Resurrection: Prayers and Poems from an Exiled Guatemalan* (Elgin, IL: Brethren Press, 1994 [1982]), 60–61.

2. Mak Dizdar, "Unwilling Warrior," in *Scar on the Stone: Contemporary Poetry from Bosnia*, ed. Chris Agee (Highgreen, England: Bloodaxe Books, 1998).

3. James Cone, *The Cross and the Lynching Tree* (Maryknoll, NY: Orbis Books, 2011), 25.

4. Thomas Merton, "Learning to Live," in *Love and Living* (New York: Bantam Books, 1979 [1965]).

5. See Merton's reflections on vocation and salvation in "Vocation and Modern Thought," in *Contemplation in a World of Action* (Notre Dame, IN: Notre Dame University Press, 1998).

6. Merton, "Learning to Live," 4. One does not have to look far for contemporary examples of the "hell" Merton speaks of. Especially since 9/11, the obsession with national security has taken extremely lethal forms in the US's conduct of the so-called War on Terror. The shaky foundations and justifications for preemptive wars, occupations, torture, and indefinite detention, and assassination by unmanned drones have all been built upon "complex artifice, systematic lying, and criminal evasions and neglects," and have spawned a variety of futile projects that are not only life-threatening to others but dangerous to the US's national soul.

7. See Jon Sobrino, "Awakening from the Sleep of Inhumanity," in *Christian Century* (April 3, 1991), 364–70.

8. Joshua Casteel, *Letters from Abu Ghraib* (Ithaca, NY: Essay Press, 2008).

9. For more information on Joshua Casteel, see the website set up for him by his mother and sisters at http://joshuacasteel.com. For several excellent video clips of Casteel speaking and being interviewed, see "Remembering Joshua Casteel" on the Iraq Veterans Against the War website at http://www.ivaw.org/blog/remembering-joshua-casteel. Also see the tribute to him by Tom Cornell, "Joshua Casteel, Conscientious Objector, RIP," *America* (August 27, 2012).

10. Casteel, *Letters from Abu Ghraib,* 50, 66.

11. Ibid., 93–94.

12. For a video of Joshua's account of this interrogation, see "How I Became a Conscientious Objector," available at http://www.youtube.com/watch?v=fM8jjqxtSpY.

13. Claribel Alegria, excerpt from "Nocturnal Visits," in *Poetry Like Bread: Poets of the Political Imagination,* ed. Martin Espada (Wilimantic, CT: Curbstone Press, 2000), 19.

14. Sobrino, "Awakening from the Sleep of Inhumanity," 1.

15. See Soelle's reflections on the ideas of Reinhold Schneider in *Dorothee Soelle: Essential Writings* (Maryknoll, NY: Orbis Books, 2006), 104.

16. Ibid., 104.

17. See Blaise Pascal, *Pensées* (Baltimore: Penguin, 1968), no. 919, 313.

18. Matilde de la Sierra, panel entitled "Telling the Truth: Torture Survivors Speak Out," Northwestern University, Evanston, Illinois, March 29–31, 2007.

19. From "Matilde and Jim: Learning to Love Again," originally aired on May 29, 2003, as a segment of Chicago Public Radio's "Love Stories" series, co-produced by Alex Kotlowitz and Amy Dorn.

20. Ibid.

21. *Beneath the Blindfold,* co-directed and co-produced by Ines Somer and Kathy Berger (2012), available at http://beneaththeblindfold.com.

22. Dorothee Soelle, *Theology for Skeptics: Reflections on God* (Minneapolis: Augsburg Fortress, 1995), 106.

23. Etty Hillesum, *An Interrupted Life* and *Letters From Westerbork* (New York: Henry Holt and Company, 1996 [1983]), 178.

INDEX